Suffer, Little Children

Max Rafferty

SUFFER, LITTLE CHILDREN

THE DEVIN-ADAIR COMPANY · NEW YORK · 1962

Contents

36733

Introduction

It has been a long, long time since the Education profession has produced a member who could write as provocatively as Max Rafferty. I don't mean "write" in the sense of theses and dissertations and textbooks. A lot of us can do that. I mean writing in terms of grace, verve, and a sort of sparkling insouciance which illuminates and vitalizes whatever it touches.

This book is the distillation of such writing skill. But if it were no more than this, it would merit only passing attention as a *tour de force*, and little else. It seems to me that it is much more. It is, among other things, a fearless, no-holds-barred attack upon what the author considers to be the great problems of Twentieth-Century Education. It is written in a prose style at once limpid and arresting. It is a style which has in it none of the moss-grown clichés and platitudes which parade in the verbal garb of "respectability."

It is not necessary to agree with Max Rafferty to enjoy this collection of his great essays on Education, gathered together now for the first time under one cover. Indeed, he would probably prefer that you do not. For many years, his concern has been to stimulate, to prod into open debate, to strike sparks which—many years later—may at last kindle into flame. Many of the principles for which he fought during the Fifties have been accepted, however reluctantly, by American Education during the Sixties. His name evokes immediate interest and discussion wherever educators are gathered together. In a very special sense, he has become the stimulus of our profession.

I do not remember any other book on Education remotely like this one. It is possible that there has never been one. To the reader discriminating enough to acquire this volume, congratulations. It is highly unlikely that the wheel of Time will turn up its successor in our lifetime.

EMERY STOOPS

Professor of Educational Administration and Supervision
University of Southern California

Los Angeles, California, 1962

Foreword

Education's first duty is to make possible the survival of
our country.

Knowledge is like a fragile but many-compartmented
Ark, precariously breasting the hostile torrent of the centuries. Each generation of Man takes what it needs from the
fifty-odd cells which its predecessors have toiled so painfully to build and to fill, and in turn erects its own, placing
within its cell all that its own time has found good. Thus,
the contents of the Ark grow with the slow accretions of
recorded history, and its gleaming cargo shines a little more
brightly each decade with the jewels which genius has so
slowly and so lovingly added.

The era in which we find ourselves is, unhappily, one of
blood and tyranny and vice. A race of faceless, godless
peasants from the steppes of Asia strives to reach across our
bodies for the prize of world dominion. They are armed
with all the sinister science which a psychopathic society
can produce. To defeat their purpose will require more
than our present brain power and our transient will. It will
demand the massed wisdom and understanding of the great
minds that have gone before us.

If this be true, it follows that the first duty of the schools
is to impart the accumulated wisdom of the race to our chil-

dren. Adjustment as an educational goal is a pricked balloon. To adjust to the twentieth century is to come to terms with madness. What is needed is the adjustment of our environment to ourselves, or rather to what we would like ourselves to be.

It is to this goal that America's schools must be committed.

We have a long way to go. . . .

▶ *What is Education?*

It exists among all mammals and most birds.

It has been the mentor and handmaiden of the human race since History began. Upon it the Future depends.

At present, it is losing its ancient race against Catastrophe.

Before we speak of the New Education, perhaps we should look back into the Past, into the infinite succession of mirrors wherein are reflected a multitude of masks. . . .

The Masks of Education

1

THE FALSE FACE is as old as history. Rigid with menace or plastic with merriment, it veils with secretive impartiality the glower of the burglar, the fanatic gaze of the witch doctor, and the lovelorn look of Harlequin. It gapes jocosely beneath the tangled curls of childhood; it rises blackly above the prognathous jaw of the headsman. How many frantic love affairs, from Juliet to Du Barry, have thriven under the glittering promise of the domino? How many anguished mourners have watched with silent tears the agile fingers of the artist fitting into the undying plaster of the death mask the immobile features of the departed?

Drama, that unexcelled catharsis for the human spirit, began with masks. Aeschylus and Sophocles designed their winged dialogue to issue resonantly from the brazen mouthpiece of the tragic mask, while Aristophanes laughed his way to immortality behind the carven grin of Comedy. Hellenic sculpture, with its placid, perfect features, aped the stage, and fashioned of Pentelic marble faces that were in all but texture masks. The gods themselves concealed their lineaments from mortal eyes with stylized scraps of cloth and thread and metal.

Legend has it that once, and only once, Chance ushered confusion into the royal house of France in the persons of twin sons, born equal and impossible heirs to the mightiest throne in Europe. Rumors of the calamity in the very throes of consummation sped on the pallid lips of hastening courtiers to the ears of Richelieu. The sinister statesman acted without delay. Standing impassively beside the moaning Anne of Austria, the Cardinal issued his directives.

"If the second child be a prince, let him be taken privily from the palace and forthwith delivered to my chamberlain. The midwife and physician I shall honor with my personal attention."

Thus, and in the course of a few hours, the second son of Louis XIII drew his first breath, only to be spirited away forever from the sight of man. The unconscious mother never knew of his existence. Still less guessed the glittering court, and even Holy Church muttered its orisons and told its beads in ignorance of the little Dauphin who had been born. Those unfortunate enough to have assisted at the accouchement received the Cardinal's reward, a speedy death.

Many years later, a certain rumor spread, a stream without apparent source, of one immured in the great pile of the Bastille, treated with all honor and loaded with luxuries commonly reserved for princes of the blood. His face was eternally covered with a vizard of metal, riveted immovably and gleaming blindly in the flickering torchlight of the gloomy fortress. The legend of the Iron Mask had come to haunt the imagination of the world.

It is no accident that the mask has always symbolized mystery. The covering of the face removes the necessity for inhibiting the emotions, and permits the release of the most primitive feelings from behind the screen of anonymity. Nothing is more popular than the masquerade party, and its reputation for both the erratic and the erotic is often well deserved. The spirit leaps exultantly, freed if only for a space from the policeman's grasp of recognition.

Yet there is one species of masking which has as its goal not the nepenthe of release but its antithesis. Richelieu's prisoner suffered behind his malignant helm not because of its shape or weight or color but because it had been fastened upon him by another, and without his consent. The very namelessness in which we revel when we can assume it at will becomes a millstone of incalculable weight when it is attached to us against our wishes. It has therefore been rightly said that the true sin against humanity lies in the forcing of an alien identity upon a fellow creature, in the molding under pressure of the immortal life stuff into a form unintended by the Creator. When we thrust a mask upon another, we commit a crime.

It is this crime which we have committed against Education. We have constrained her to wear not one but a succession of masks.

THE PRIMITIVE MASK

When Tegumai, the Neolithic hunter, took his son into the trackless forest, he taught him survival. The trick of the deadfall, the cunning of the snare, the lore of the bow and spear were imparted one by one by the Old Man to the younger. Whether he taught the chipping of one stone against another or the curing of deerskin, the primitive instructor wasted no breath, brooked no argument. Generations of trial and error had condensed knowledge into a package, the compactness and simplicity of which has been unmatched to this day. Each lesson was driven home by fear and seared upon the memory by necessity.

A contemplative Tegumai, had one existed, might well have congratulated himself upon his success as a teacher.

"Education," he would have concluded inescapably, "is a Craft."

THE CLASSICAL MASK

The peripatetic philosophers, strolling past the columns of the Stoa, discussed justice and truth and honor as delightful abstractions. The youthful Alcibiades, drunken and ribald, attached himself to the grotesque figure of Socrates as today our teenagers fasten upon some illiterate, guitar-strumming hillbilly, and with the same motive: entertainment.

"Oh, Socrates," he blurted, "truly, I had rather be in your company than at a banquet."

Learning was a delight to the ancient world, a splendid challenging of the mind. Better than new wine was the intoxication of new ideas. Geometry was taught as an intriguing game, the great epics as fascinating fiction. It was no accident that music ranked level with mathematics and astronomy in the quadrivium. To the ancients, all were equally amusing.

Plato, lifting his white head from the gentlemanly circle of the Academy, smiles at us down the centuries.

"Education, of course, is a Recreation."

THE MEDIEVAL MASK

The typical teacher of the Middle Ages was St. Thomas Aquinas. In his attempt to reconcile the logic of Aristotle with the Gospels, he embodied all that was earnest combined with all that was subtle of a period which glorified both qualities. Instruction for a thousand years had one purpose, and one only: the greater glorification of God. It existed to bear witness to the revealed Truth. The teacher taught facts and attitudes with the Kingdom of Heaven constantly in mind. No branch of learning was justified unless it contributed in some measure to the saving of the soul.

Alcuin, great teacher of the sons of Charlemagne, might have summed up the thinking of the Scholastics thus: "We study grammar that we may better comprehend the Scriptures, drawing that we may present the fall and redemption of man in graphic form for all to understand, music that we may glorify God in the language of the blessed angels."

Latest blooming but most splendid flower of medieval education was the Society of Jesus. Tutoring in a dozen courts, proselyting in a hundred wildernesses, the Jesuits brought to fruition ten centuries of God-centered instruction. These stark, black-robed enthusiasts had no slightest doubt of their mission. Their chant still echoes in a vastly different world:

"Education is Evangelism."

THE RENAISSANCE MASK

Cellini, shaping the jeweled miracles that made his name immortal, quipped that he was in love with Venus and Apollo. Lorenzo de' Medici, embarked upon the great collection of classic art that has forever coupled magnificence with his name, regretted only that his time was not contemporary with that of Phidias and Apelles, and forced himself to be reluctantly content with Michelangelo.

Erasmus said of the Humanists, "They seek not to center earthly life in God, but rather in Man, after the fashion of the antique Greeks and Romans."

Scrolls that had not been opened for a millennium were brought to light by eager clerks and scholars. Attic Greek, a lost language for a thousand years, was smuggled into a still barbaric Europe from a crumbling Byzantium, and catalyzed the worship of the past into one white-hot blaze of longing for a beauty and a learning that had been forgotten. The present was contemptible, the future unpredictable. The past alone was precious and unique, shimmering like St. Brendan's Isle above the boundaries of the attainable. A host of struggling artists and ink-stained students sent up the nostalgic murmur:

"Education is the loving resurrection of the Past. It is Research."

THE NINETEENTH-CENTURY MASK

Newtonian physics was beginning visibly to break down. Darwin and Huxley were thundering in the wings, and cracks were starting to appear in the very foundation of Things As They Are. Yet the Age of Victoria strove desperately to cling to those twin idols, Order and Appearance. It is no coincidence that in this era Education made her first appearance as a mass phenomenon. The established order invoked her in a vain effort to hold back the tide of the future, but, like the genie in the bottle, she refused to keep the shape in which she had been envisioned by her discoverer.

The attempt was made, however, and made vigorously. It took the form of instruction in the harmless fields of dead languages, ancient history, theology, and literature. Science in the people's schools had an uphill battle; it tended to discourage orthodoxy. Euclidean geometry was welcomed as an intellectual toy, but the newfangled notions of differential calculus and space-time continuum mathematics were taboo. Law was the proper study of the gentleman; it rested on precedent, and abhorred novelty. Classes were taught to memorize, to recite, and to indite, seldom to think.

These worshipers of the status quo regarded the instruction of their children with mixed emotions. In the proper hands, they assured themselves, it would be quite safe, perhaps even mildly beneficial. They settled their cravats and rattled their teacups with apprehensive assurance.

"Education," they told themselves in well-bred accents, "is Rote."

THE TWENTIETH-CENTURY MASK

Enter the Age of Imbalance, with dissonance and the shrieking of gears. For the first time, the masses took over the reins instead of merely supplying the horsepower. Never before had Education been so honored; never before had she been so prolific. Her temples polkadotted the land and, after centuries of neglect, she now found herself reviled for her failure to supply immediate answers to unprecedented questions. The innocent victim of a popular dichotomy, she became at once the object of adoration and the butt of ridicule.

In their perplexity, her devotees turned with relief to the new spirit of investigation and classification that walked abroad, altering old concepts and uprooting cherished beliefs with the blind and impartial force of the hurricane.

"Surely," they told one another, "in an age which piles marvel upon marvel and bases all its garish superstructure upon a foundation of constant flux, Education must also undergo a metamorphosis."

And so they forced upon her still another mask. This, like the one that cast its unseen shadow against the gray walls of the Bastille so many years before, is of burnished metal, but its form is vastly different. Cast in the shape of a machine, the twentieth-century mask glows with cold electronic fires and pulses with myriad tiny, moving parts. These bear such labels as "retroactive inhibitions," "standard deviations," and "partial correlations." The mask is never quite the same for two moments in a row, but somehow manages to contain the St. Vitus leaping of its shifting cogs within the confines of its matrix. The contours of the mask are streamlined and utilitarian; they mirror the eternal minuet of stimulus and response and the frigid logic of sociological trends. The features breathe an icy confidence, a satisfied certainty in the right answers.

Above the clicking of their tabulating machines and the rustle of the rats in their mazes, the white-clad acolytes of twentieth-century learning gaze emotionlessly out of a thousand television screens.

"Education," they enunciate precisely, "is a Science."

The cream of the jest is, of course, that Education is simultaneously all and none of these things. Like the blind men and the elephant, humanity has oscillated from one aspect of Education to another throughout recorded history, each time identifying her in accents of surprise with a different one of her innumerable attributes.

Education is not a Craft, although she teaches many crafts. She is not a Recreation, though she makes constructive recreation possible. Neither is she Research nor yet Memorization, regardless of how large these worthy functions may bulk in the educational pattern as successive generations approach and pass.

In our own time, the identification of Education with Science is understandable. We have put all our eggs for the future into one basket labeled *Science*, and with our child-like faith in the magic of names, we have attempted to crowd Education into the back door of the laboratory so that she might be revivified and transmuted by the "big medicine" which clusters around the name of Science.

But Education is not Science.

Massive injections of psychology and sociology and statistical methods do not produce a science. The brandishing of fairy wands in the form of fruity phrases such as "on-going," "forward-looking," and "meaningfully relevant" will not, despite our fervent supplications, confer the sterile mantle of Science upon the shoulders of our profession. The irony of the whole affair is that we should ever wish for her to become a science. Science is a continuing search for knowledge, a perpetual balancing of postulates with proofs. Education is so much more than this that for its practitioners to rest content with Science makes as little sense as did the smugness of our Victorian forebears with the ultimate utility of Rote.

If Education were a Science and nothing more, we would not be worrying about pupil attitudes and creativeness and imagination. The trick of Science lies in the artful elimination or the minimizing of variable factors, but Education deals with nothing but variables. The statistics upon which we set such store melt into slush when confronted with the stubborn nonconformity of the individual. The laws which mean so much to Science and which, like those of the Medes and the Persians, alter not, are strait jackets when applied to Education. Science by its very nature must regard the individual as one out of a swarming mass of units which combine to prove a theorem. To Education, the individual is the be-all and the end-all of the profession.

The educator should approach his class not as the chemist appraises his retorts nor the astronomer his nebulae but rather as the conductor confronts his symphony orchestra. From the breathless whispering of the strings, from the clarion peals of the brass, from the muted thunder of the percussion, the conductor will weave the very fabric of great music, threaded throughout with the polychromatic strands of his own genius. Even so will the teacher evoke from the myriad experiences and abilities of his pupils the chords which, laced and interwoven with something of himself, will ring grandly in the harmony of life. There is a mingling of moods, an elusive interplay of spiritual counterpoint implicit in the teaching process which marks the closest human approach to the phenomenon of symbiosis. In its highest form it approximates creation, a far cry indeed from Science, which unleashes the forces of the mind upon matter to transform and to refashion but never to create.

This is an eternal verity. It has always been true. It always will be. It had the same solid ring of reality in the days of Pericles that it will have for our remote descendants. We must train our teachers as a sculptor is trained, not as a physicist. They must think like poets, not like statisticians. For they are dealing not with things like the chemists, nor with bodies like the physicians, nor yet with minds alone like the psychologists. To them and to us is reserved the splendid privilege of fashioning and nurturing those coruscating and iridescent entities called personalities, transient as glancing sunbeams but more lasting than the granite of our hills. It is at once the most precious and most dangerous duty entrusted by mankind to men. It can be properly consummated only by stripping the last of the disfiguring masks from the lovely face of Education, that we and those who follow us may look on beauty bare.

Education is an Art.

► *But for a generation and more, the great Art was thrust aside. In its place, the scarecrow figure of Pragmatic Progressivism rode tall in the saddle, brandishing the brittle lance of Behavioristic Psychology and armored with the invulnerable reputation of John Dewey.*

It was the Era of the Gimmick, the Age of Adjustment, the Period of the Peer Group. The smoke of its altars rose over the corpses of subject matter and discipline, and in the smoky columns the scarecrow loomed ever larger. Its form began imperceptibly to change, to darken, until. . . .

Suffer, Little Children

2

IT WAS THE final agony for the great city. Despite the patient subtleties of Hannibal and the frenzied trumpetings of the great war elephants, Destiny and Carthage had at last come face to face. A hundred battles and a hundred thousand dead had led only to this: the Roman legions thundering at the gates, and Famine gripping Punic bellies in the seething ant hill that was the city. The fairest daughters of the oligarchy had long since pledged their lives to Ashtoreth and their lustrous locks to be shorn and braided and woven into bowstrings for the black Numidian archers who manned the crumbling walls. The fat and hook-nosed merchant princes had lumbered forth to bargain with the grim invader, to offer bribes of gold and slaves and Tyrian purple. They had remained to decorate the ubiquitous crosses which dotted the open plain about the dying city. Their piping screams mingled with the ribald taunts of their tormentors and with the whistling and thudding of the great siege engines.

The shape of Ate, that fiery-faced and typically Roman goddess of destruction, brooded visibly over the hovels and palaces of the doomed metropolis.

In the exact center of the city, a vast and sinister form reared itself against the African sky. Cast in gleaming bronze, it squatted on its haunches leering at the teeming hordes that sobbed and surged about its massive pedestal, spurred on to their desperate worship by the howling of their priests. On this, the last night of the city's life, Carthage swarmed and groveled at the feet of Moloch. Lit with the glow of myriad torches, the god seemed slowly to shine with some inner radiance, and, as the night grew older and the cachinnations of the mob more frenzied, the slitted eyes of Moloch cast two beams of lurid crimson through the murk. Within the brazen belly of the god, his priests had kindled great fires which heated the huge idol to incandescence and caused the obscene features to shimmer fiendishly in the waves of heat.

An inclined runway led from the ground before the god to the door which now gaped open just below his navel. Up this ramp, driven by hippopotamus-hide whips in the hands of the foaming priests, stumbled and crept the children of Carthage. Babes in the arms of their older brothers and sisters, toddlers scarce able to lisp their mothers' names, wide-eyed little maids and sturdy boys, they went to the embrace of Moloch. They were garlanded with flowers, decked with jewels, and mad with fear. Below and gazing up at the shrinking victims genuflected their tearless elders, stabbing the night air with their shrieks to the god, imploring that the sacrifice be accepted and the destruction of the city averted.

One by one, sobbing and crying to their unhearing parents, the little ones were prodded and whipped to the edge of the runway, where they gazed down into Hell itself before they toppled pitifully into the molten bowels of the grinning god. The stench of burning flesh reached even to the nostrils of the besieging Romans, who paused, white-faced, beside their rams and catapults. Above the roar of maddened thousands, the red-hot countenance of Moloch glowed satiated, and promised victory upon the morrow.

The next day, the Romans sacked the city.

All the Carthaginians who had watched their children broil were tossed screaming from the city walls, entombed in flaming buildings, or spitted like geese upon the short swords of the legionairies. Moloch himself was thrown down, shattered into fragments, and spat upon.

Carthage was destroyed as no other city has ever been destroyed.

"Who shall offend one of these little ones," said a Greater than Moloch, "it were better for him that a mill-stone were hanged around his neck, and that he were drowned in the depths of the sea."

Never did a city so richly deserve its fate.

The great wheel of history has turned ponderously full-circle since the Punic Wars. A happier time for children dawned a century ago, and in that Golden Age a whole new pantheon of youthful gods and goddesses came down from Mount Olympus and made old Earth a magic place for boys and girls.

Wilfred of Ivanhoe rode stirrup to stirrup with Cœur de Leon, and the evil hold of Torquilstone burned eternal witness to the power of youth and goodness. Laughing and shouting in the same great company rode Arthur with his Table Round, forever splintering their lances in the cause of right, and leading forth the massed chivalry of France

came Bayard, without fear and without reproach. A little
to one side strode Christian, arms folded and eyes fixed
steadfastly upon the Eternal City, but always with his good
sword ready for the onset of Apollyon. Roistering and
invincible swaggered Porthos, Athos and Aramis, with the
young D'Artagnan, ever ready to draw those magic blades,
the wonder of the world, for truth and glory and the
Queen. The horn of Roland echoed through the pass at
Roncesvalles, and somehow caught and mingled with the
blast of Robin Hood, calling down the misty years upon
his merry men of Sherwood.

Were not these fit gods for the children of mankind?

Apart and in a merry company leaped and played the
Child Immortals. Hand in hand with long-haired Alice
walked Christopher Robin, bright eyes alert for talking
rabbits and greedy little bears. Sturdy Jim Hawkins
counted his pieces of eight and chaffed with Captain Flint,
while young Tom Sawyer kept a wary lookout for the
menace that was Injun Joe. A battered raft floated to
immortality upon the broad bosom of the Father of Waters,
and Huck became the apotheosis of all boys everywhere.
Meg, Jo and Beth chattered gaily to Amy, and Dorothy
skipped arm in arm with the Scarecrow down the yellow
brick road.

When in any age have children had such shining
exemplars?

It remained for our own generation to turn its back upon
the heroes of the children and to mold a twentieth-century
version of Moloch. His new name is Utilitarianism, and his
priests are the pragmatists. Their ritual involves the endless
repetition of the mystic words "adjustment to environ-

ment." Their goal is the destruction of all that cannot be statistically demonstrated, the immolation of fancy and fantasy and all that makes men different from the brutes. Even the nursery rhymes which have come down to us from time immemorial have been pronounced "reactionary" and "sordid." Hansel and Gretel have been dehydrated and neutralized to the status of Cincinnati children on a Sunday-school picnic, and Jack the Giant-Killer to a schoolboy swatting flies. Everything that was fearful and wonderful and glamorous has been leveled off to the lowest common denominator.

Ulysses and Penelope have been replaced by Dick and Jane in the textbooks of our schools. The quest for the Golden Fleece has been crowded out by the visit of Tom and Susan to the zoo. The deeds of the heroes before Troy are now passé, and the peregrinations of the local milkman as he wends his way through the stodgy streets and littered alleys of Blah City are deemed worthy of numberless pages in our primers. The sterile, stone-age culture of the Pueblo Indians looms large in our curriculum but the knightly Crusaders are ignored. Jackie pursues his insipid goal of a ride in the district garbage truck with good old crotchety Mr. Jones while the deathless ride of Paul Revere goes unwept, unhonored and unsung. It is interesting, and certainly significant, that modern education has deliberately debunked the hero to make room for the jerk. The lofty exception to the rank and file, whom all of us could envy and emulate, has been compelled to give way to the Great Mediocrity, the synthesis of all that is harmless and safe and banal among us.

Today, after two thousand years, again we worship

Moloch. We sacrifice our children to him, and ululate his praises while all that is bright and promising in the generation which will follow us droops in the hot breath of the commonplace.

Moloch today is fashioned in the blasphemous image of Ourselves.

He is Daddy in the second-grade readers who comes mincing home with his eternal briefcase from his meaningless day in his antiseptic office just in time to pat Jip the dog and carry blonde little Laurie into the inevitable white bungalow on his stylishly padded shoulders.

He is Mommy in the third-grade books, always silk-stockinged and impeccable after a day spent over the electric range, with never a cross word on her carefully made-up lips and never an idea in her empty head.

He is Dick and Jane and Tom and Susan, and all the insufferable nonentities who clutter up the pages of our texts with their vapid ditherings about humdrum affairs which could never be of conceivable interest to anyone above the level of an idiot.

The crimson eyes of Moloch glare out at us from a thousand courses of study wherein pyramids are built in miniature but Egypt is ignored, igloos constructed but the vast panorama of the Northland forgotten, Kachina masks contrived but the place of the Indian in American history relegated to the realm of the unimportant. The voice of Moloch resounds throughout the land, averring in its oleaginous Teachers College accent that only the child's felt needs must be met, that memorization is a sin against the Holy Ghost, and that homework went out with the mustache cup. Haroun-al-Raschid, he whispers, is fascist, Tom Swift a rapacious capitalist, and Charlemagne a bloody old medievalist. The wars we fought were selfish wars; the people we died to free were pawns upon the chessboard of economic determinism; the precious documents that milestone our liberties were strait jackets fitted to the proletariat.

The children are being ushered along a facile runway, paved ever so smoothly with construction units and field trips, socializations and sharings, assemblies and group dynamics. The priests who prod them forward are hot-eyed, with telltale patches of saliva gathering in the corners of their mouths; they are devotees of the mediocre, which they worship under the sacred alias of Democratic Methods. They have been crammed to the craw with educationism, as long ago the zombie followers of the Old Man of the Mountain were stuffed with hashish. Their temples are the great universities which marble the land, stretching out their thousand campaniles to a Heaven of Demonstrable Utility and turning out swarms of neophytes each year to preach the gospel of Group Adaptation. Their secret crypts and inner sanctums are the graduate schools, which confer upon the masters of the cult certain cabalisms and charms in the guise of critiques and seminars, but which avoid any tinge of concern with literary or cultural refinements as a Moslem would a pork chop.

At the end of the runway lies, as it lay twenty centuries ago, a special kind of hell. We have improved somewhat upon the Carthaginians in the kind of fire which we provide and in the special types of fuel with which we stoke the flames. Just as our idol is no longer of massy bronze, so also is our conflagration one of the spirit rather than the flesh. But it burns deep.

It scorches genius.

It sears creative imagination to the bone.

It withers nonconformity.

All the pleasant flights of fancy which have brightened the horizons of our young for decades past—Peter Pan and Cinderella, Hercules and Thor—are grist for this monstrous, flaming mill. The slag and ashes are later shoveled into shape and substituted for the shimmering originals, ashes in the inane persons of Bill the Delivery Boy or Mr. Kindly, the Tugboat Operator.

Words that America has treasured as a rich legacy, that have sounded like trumpet calls above the clash of arms and the fury of debate, are fading from the classrooms, and so from life itself. "Liberty and Union, now and forever, one and inseparable. . . ." "I only regret that I have but one life to give for my country. . . ." "Millions for defense, but not one cent for tribute. . . ." Search for these golden phrases in vain today in the textbooks of too many of our schools, in the hearts and minds of too many of our children. The golden words are gone, and in their place brain-numbing accounts of the nation's second-class mail service or units on the trucking industry and Highway 66. We must all, you see, grow up to be mailmen or truckers. We have no need of Websters, nor of Nathan Hales.

If education is not to hand down from generation to generation the priceless treasures of the ages, what indeed is it to do? How can it justify its own existence? Can it be that our great goal is to teach our sons and daughters to twitch in convulsive tremors of adjustment to the ever-shifting kaleidoscope of modern life? Can we justify the billions that we spend if the results are to be found largely in the areas of finger painting, folk dancing, and the writing of business letters? Is it possible that Rousseau and Pestalozzi, Plato and Barnard have come at last to this tragic conclusion of their dreams and hopes?

O my brothers in this game of blind-man's buff with children's lives, let us strike off the blindfolds. Let us look long and earnestly at what we are doing.

We are teaching trivia.

Do not take my word. If you find the dose unpalatable, if you balk at the nauseous implications, try your pupils.

Watch the abler ones grow dull and apathetic, bored and lackluster, as they yawn and watch the clock over the stupid adventures of Muk-Muk the Eskimo Boy or Little Pedro from Argentina. Then, suddenly, as though opening an enchanted window upon a radiant pageant, give them the story of the wrath of Achilles. Let them stand with Casabianca upon the burning deck. Trek with them in spirit to the Yukon, and with glorious Buck let them answer the call of the wild. Place them upon the shot-swept shrouds of the *Bonhomme Richard*, and let them thrill to those words flashing like a rapier out of our past, "I have not yet begun to fight." Kneel with them behind the cotton bales at New Orleans with Andy Jackson at their side as the redcoats begin to emerge from the mist of the Louisiana swamps and the sullen guns of Lafitte begin to pound.

Watch their faces.

See the eyes brighten and the spirits ruffle. See the color

come, the backs straighten, the arms go up. They dream, they live, they glow.

This is teaching. This is what you trained to do. You have done what any teacher worth his salt would mortgage his future to achieve, and you have set the ardent, selfless joy of learning flaming in those eager faces.

Thus you may hurl the eternal lie into the teeth of those who decry the significance of subject matter, who sneer at history and poetry and mythology and all those magical creations of the human mind which have raised man to a place a little lower than the gods.

Let us lift our heads. Let us say to these diluters of curricula, these emasculators of texts, these mutilators of our past, "We have had enough of you. The world is weary of you. The stage is ready for new actors. With your jargon of behaviorism and Gestalt and topological vectors and maturation levels, you have muddied the clear waters of childhood long enough. You have told us to teach the whole child, but you have made it impossible to teach him anything worth learning. Little by little you have picked the meat from the bones of Education and replaced it with Pablum. You have done your best to produce a race of barely literate savages."

These things we can say, and we can follow words with deeds.

What say you, brothers?

Shall we continue to shovel the children into the maw of Moloch?

► *The children were not the only sufferers. The nihilistic leveling that was so much a part of the Progressive credo infected the very essence of Education itself, in the person of the classroom teacher. Since subject matter was ephemeral, unreal, why should the teacher know anything? Intellectualism became suspect. Insistence upon standards declined as the teacher's own standards dwindled. The teacher, it seemed, was fated to become just another worker on the treadmill of the New Social Order. . . .*

The Philistines

3

EDUCATION IS THE Don Quixote of the professions. Like the Knight of the Rueful Countenance, educators love to go roaming about the countryside looking for trouble. The more formidable the windmill, the more menacingly it looms above us, the more enthusiastically do we level our lances and spur on our steeds. It seems to matter little to us that several of these windmills belong properly to other parties, and that their ultimate disposal will depend almost entirely upon events and factors over which educators as a group have little or no direct control. This tilting with vast national issues originating in causes outside our own bailiwick may be exhilarating, but it can result eventually in our occupying the same dunce stool reserved by popular opinion for the lovable loony of La Mancha.

Other professions appear to resist more successfully this urge to go crusading off the reservation. Our friends the physicians seem to feel that they have their hands full trying to cure cancer without teeing off on the Arab-Israeli dispute, and their journals stick fairly close to such medical enigmas as heart disease and arthritis instead of haring off after low-cost housing or Chester Bowles. About the only time the medics got tangled up with a controversy stemming from a basically extraprofessional source was the abortive attempt to discourage health insurance. The result was predictable; they were clobbered.

Lawyers similarly avoid pretty well the temptation to be indiscriminately nosy, confining their convention speeches to such safely legal topics as the jury trial for criminal contempt and the caliber of juridical competence displayed by Chief Justice Warren. In fact, the members of our great sister professions concentrate their efforts upon setting their own houses in order, while at the same time keeping their mouths shut about matters outside their chosen province.

Our own profession is a different matter. Educators seldom stop to consider whether the particular cause which they have seen fit to espouse is susceptible to solution *within the profession*. If it is not, of course, then they are wasting their time as educators, though no doubt enjoying a certain amount of forensic exercise in the capacity of private citizen. It is no accident that the two most highly publicized issues in education today are federal aid and racial integration. Both are headlined in our publications and orated about at our conventions. Neither is a professional problem in the true sense of the word.

Take integration, for instance. Here is an enormous spaghetti tangle of historical trends, sauced with complicated economic factors and liberally peppered with emotional bias. Its roots are anchored back before the first establishment of public education in this country. Its final outcome will affect every man, woman, and child in the nation. The schools are caught up in the whistling tunnel of this awesome tornado and swirled back and forth by the cross-current of violence which mark its course across the embattled South. It should be obvious to everyone that here is a colossal proposition involving every segment of our population; it will not be worked out for many years, and then only by well-timed and continuing efforts on the part of the nation as a whole. Does anyone seriously believe that the solution to this mighty headache lies within our profession?

Yet many of our best educational brains are grappling desperately with this giant, like so many Jacobs tackling black angels. They are writing, talking, even breathing and sleeping integration instead of devoting their badly needed intelligences to solving those puzzles to which Education alone can supply the key. It is already possible to trace the path of the integration whirlwind by the strewn professional corpses of educators who should never have been out challenging the twister in the first place. Many a man now busily sounding off on this ponderous enigma is destined to find himself eventually in the exact position of the reckless tyro who climbed into the ring with the champ without bothering to arrange for seconds who could apply the wet towels.

Federal aid, to cite another example of this sort of thing, will never be achieved as the result of efforts originating wholly within the education profession. This should be apparent by now, in view of the political punching bag into which the issue has been recently refashioned, despite the anguished protest of every educator in the land. If it ever was a proper item on the professional agenda, federal aid ceased to qualify as soon as it became fouled up with formulas and enmeshed in congressional logrolling. It may be successfully argued that educators should tell the people, over and over again if necessary, that more money is needed urgently if Education is to continue to make decent nation-wide progress. What surely cannot be logically claimed, however, is that we educators should transform ourselves into fiscal authorities and legislative lobbyists in order to do something completely outside our sphere of competence, and in which we exhibit such slight genius that we run the risk of becoming a laughing stock.

All this is not to say that the profession should not take a stand on many great national and world contentions which are allied only remotely to Education. It should and it does. The point is that we should attack most vigorously the enemies who are closest to us. Our own back yards are so cluttered, our own home-grown problems so badly in need of weeding and cultivating that when we disperse our energies and scatter our fire we betray our own calling. We must follow the principle of first things first, or chance seeing the profession eroded visibly out from under us, like the iceberg which has invaded tropic seas.

There is really only one great problem in American Education today; all the others stem from it, and will be on the way toward solution when it is solved. This is the tragedy of declining standards.

The cry will now go up:

"What can this fellow mean? Never have our schools been so safe and comfortable, our tools and equipment so elaborate, our graduate schools so crowded. More money is being spent than ever before to make Education a worthy handmaiden and interpreter to the Atomic Age. Where, then, are these declining standards?"

All this is true. Moreover, in several other spheres, standards have risen remarkably, and are still going up. Comprehensive physical examinations are now required for all school employees in many states, and there is less likelihood than at any time in the past that diseased or mentally disturbed persons will be in daily contact with our children. Moral standards have always been higher among the members of our profession than of any other save the ministry, and with the rise of fingerprinting as a concomitant of qualification, men and women with criminal backgrounds are virtually excluded from positions in the schools. Teachers and administrators are better looking and better dressed than those of only a generation ago. They possess far more degrees and credentials than did their predecessors. How can standards be said to be declining in the light of such powerful evidence to the contrary?

The standards I am talking about are intellectual.

In the field of cultural attainments, and in this alone, the upgrading process which has been so marked in other areas of the profession has been conspicuous by its absence. Our teachers, taken as a great totality, today know more about mental hygiene than those who went before, but less about the English language. They are far more at ease in the field of handicrafts, but far less so in discussion of historical figures or events. They have more instructional techniques at their disposal than did their forebears, but fewer resources in the realms of literature and art.

Too many educators can no longer write a paragraph correctly.

Too many cannot spell a variety of words in common use.

Too many make gross errors of grammar in their daily speech.

Too many are lost when the conversation turns to cultural subjects.

I have heard it argued that deterioration in the field of general culture, if it is actually occurring, is unimportant. "After all, if the teacher can turn the child into an integrated member of a democratic society," it is said, "that is the significant thing. The child's ability to make optimum adjustments, to solve meaningful problems, and to work creatively with his hands are the major goals of modern teaching. Whatever subject matter is selected to implement these objectives should always be considered the means to an end, never as a goal in itself."

It is sloppy thinking of this type which has plunged us into the dilemma in which the profession now finds itself. Young men and women who have learned to love learning for its own sake, to revere the great masterworks of the past which have been preserved for us through much travail and many difficulties, to dream of handing on the torch from generation to generation, have always formed the strong foundation of our profession. This is no longer true.

The torch has been put out; indeed, they have been told with authority that no torch exists, nor ever did.

Above the proscenium of a noted western university auditorium are blazoned in gold the great words of Josiah Royce: "Education is learning to use the tools which the race has found indispensable." In too many of our centers of learning, this sentiment has been relegated to the dust-heap of antiquity, and in its place there glisten the *mene, mene, tekel, upharsin* of the pragmatists: "Education is learning to adjust to one's environment."

Small comfort here for the eager neophyte who believes that the child should be taught to rise above his environment, to alter it, to remold it closer to the heart's desire! No wonder this intellectual elite, for centuries the backbone of the profession, is now deserting it, reluctantly and with many backward glances but irrevocably. Science is the richer for their disillusionment; so is industry; so are the arts. And recently, to everyone's vast surprise, articles have begun to find their way into educational publications deploring the loss of able college graduates to other careers than Education, and hinting at the horrid statistics which relegate the teacher trainee to the bottom of the college ability totem pole. Money is the cause glibly assigned to the loss—money, at a time when teacher salaries are rising more rapidly than at any time in two thousand years!

In the terminology of television, let's face it. A profession which attaches little or no value to the culture of the past, which makes a fetish of fuzzy catchwords like "in-groupness" and "peer status," and which derogates every kind of knowledge to which a "practical" value cannot be attached is not going to attract the same combination of the idealistic and the learned which once manned the ramparts of Education in its unceasing battle with the forces of ignorance. Instead, it will attract the opportunist, the faddist, the inferior mind. Education is becoming less and less a profession and more and more an occupation. The recent rise of trade unionism among our teachers is no coincidence. Unless the trend is reversed, sometime within the next generation teaching will be equated with skilled labor.

We are replacing the zealous shock troops with the sluggish mercenaries.

It is not only the teacher who has changed. The school administrator is undergoing some rather drastic transformation himself. In America formerly, as in Europe still, the schoolmaster acted as the repository of whatever culture was to be found in the community.

A former student of mine who became a paratrooper during World War II and found himself stationed in various European countries made it an invariable custom to seek out a typical resident of each town his outfit liberated, and ask him to name the village's three most successful citizens. Almost always, he recalled, he was given the same three titles: the *maire*, or burgomaster; the *curé* or priest; and the schoolmaster. The last had achieved his high eminence predominantly through his reputation as the town's most erudite inhabitant. How many Americans, confronted by the same question, would come up with the name of the local principal or superintendent of schools?

The administrator has become a businessman, concerned with matters of assessed valuation, supply purchasing, and public relations. He can draw up a budget, engineer a property deal, or placate a taxpayer. All too seldom, alas, can he paraphrase Milton, summarize Boyle's Law, or discuss the Wars of the Roses. Such skills, formerly possessed by schoolmen as a *sine qua non* of the position, placed them in a class somewhat apart from the run-of-the-mill merchant or banker. A barely discernible aura of prestige surrounded the educator, and did much to offset low pay and inadequate facilities.

Today, the schoolman is reaping the reward of his long-term effort to become a businessman; he has finally become one, and is accepted as such by a community made up largely of businessmen. He is one of the boys now, and much good may it do him. His old prestige is one with Nineveh and Tyre. Unfortunately, his salary does not come even close to matching those of his back-slapping commercial compeers, so from any standpoint he has bartered his birthright for a mess of rather diluted pottage.

If the blame for the cultural downgrading of the profession can be said to rest with any single agency or group, it must be attached unhesitatingly to the teacher-training institutions of the nation. With few exceptions, they have failed to recognize the need for the educator to be the cultural leader of the community. In awarding advanced degrees, they have stressed the "how" rather than the "what." They have almost literally welcomed all comers into the profession without stopping to examine intelligence, literacy, or erudition, until it can be seriously said that anyone above the moron level who possesses sufficient time, money, and perseverance can get a master's degree in education from any institution in the land that offers it.

Educators now collect college units the way housewives collect green stamps. The units, like the courses they symbolize, mean nothing to the average school person; when pyramided according to the rules, however, they pay off in degrees, credentials, or advances on the salary schedule. An educational numbers racket of this sort, glorifying the material goal at the expense of true learning, can guarantee only one added skill to its followers at the end of the long, long trail: they will be able to count.

Closely allied with the colleges in the perpetuation of this modern educational philistinism, or "creeping meatballism," are the several state departments of education. By the simple device of multiplying methods course requirements for the various school credentials, they have made it so unlikely as to be almost unheard of for the average educator to take subject-matter courses designed to lessen his cultural deficiencies. By deliberately failing to set up minimum standards of achievement for all licensed educators in such fields as literature, history, art, and science, they tacitly infer that it is more important for a teacher to know how to construct a unit on "The Home and the Community" than to be able to distinguish between Andrew Jackson and Andrew Johnson or to scan a line of poetry. The educator is thus caught between the Scylla of the training institution and the Charybdis of the state department, a plight made ineffably more poignant by the fact that the poor devil's educational background has made it extremely unlikely that he has ever heard of either Scylla or Charybdis in any connection.

Fortunately for the future, this centralization of responsibility for the disease carries with it the seeds of the cure. Should the time ever come when Education should wish to rechart her course and steer by the stars again instead of by the false St. Elmo's fire of pragmatism, the means will be at hand. College boards of regents are, after all, susceptible both to logic and to public opinion. State departments of education are creatures of the state, and may be changed in character and in direction at the behest of the state. Strong and able men in key positions, such as university deans and state superintendents, can dig new channels through which proper instruction can flow. Indeed, in certain institutions and in several states this is already going on.

It is ironic that a great part of the criticism now being directed against the weaknesses present in modern education is coming from university and college professors. It would seem that our friends the dons have finally been confronted with some of the cruder products of the system, on a level hitherto populated by a gratifyingly selective segment of the *genus* student, and, in short, they are appalled. Their Macedonian cries are, however, directed against the public schools of the land; they assume that the problem originates and is responsive to treatment on a lower educational level than their own.

They are wrong.

The theory which justifies the current lowering of standards was conceived, delivered, and incubated on a college campus.

The philosophy which denies eternal verities, glorifies the immediately useful, and decries learning for the sake of learning originated with a university professor, and was spread through the land by university men and women.

More than any other, the entity which perpetuates this philosophy today is the American university.

In many cases, our friend the professor writes his diatribes against the public schools from an ivory tower situated in close proximity to another from which certain of his colleagues are busily sending forth each year teachers imbued with the identical principles against which he is protesting. The professor's problem lies on his own campus, if he but knew it. Let him set it aright, and in the fullness of time all will yet be well.

For the great question comes down to this: are we to unravel our own Gordian knot, or are we to wait until some outside Alexander comes to cut it for us? The former course is difficult but full of hope for the future, the latter easy but fraught with peril.

In the event that we decide to meet the challenge ourselves, as a profession, the way is open:

We can raise standards by requiring minimum academic criteria for admission to candidacy for advanced degrees in Education.

We can raise standards by insisting that undergraduates enrolled in an Education major be exposed to more and stiffer academic subjects.

We can raise standards by persuading our state departments of education to substitute selected courses in history and English, art and science, for certain subjects now required which, to put it charitably, are of limited value.

We can raise standards by providing that our would-be administrators be compelled to pass cultural tests at least as comprehensive as are the examinations which they must now hurdle in such areas as psychology and curriculum.

Unless we do these things, or something very like them, we shall continue to watch our caliber diminish, our reputation wane, and our influence fade. Money, that patent remedy for so many ills, cannot cure this one; in and by itself, money cannot raise standards for us. Only we ourselves can prescribe and carry through the necessary treatment. For, in a sense, all of us are guilty of the thing which has come to pass.

The Philistines are still strong among us.

They scoff at standards. They deride the importance of culture.

They stand squarely athwart the path which leads upward to the golden highlands of literacy and scholarship.

They represent a sullen, leaden menace to us all.

Anyone for Operation Bootstrap?

► *Finally, it got to be a joke. To the mythical observer from Mars, it must have looked like a scene from Alice in Wonderland. Educators spoke and acted like embodiments of Revealed Certainty, standing foursquare upon ground that even then was eroding beneath them. There was an element of hilarious unreality about the whole affair, considering what was to happen to the creaking, straining structure of Education when an angry nation awoke one morning to find Sputnik riding American sky space. . . .*

I HOPE THAT you are as partial to fairy stories as I am, because I have here a collection of seven lulus. They may not hark back quite as far as *Rapunzel*, nor yet be quite as enshrouded in the mists of antiquity as *Jack the Giant-Killer*, but they are quite elderly enough to have rooted themselves like so many impacted molars in the folklore of our profession.

All of you will recognize these old myths immediately. We imbibed them like mother's milk from the abundantly flowing bosoms of our training teachers, our professors of education, and the richly maternal experts of the various state departments of education. They were pounded into us the same way that the Homeric legends were hammered into the heads of little Greek boys two thousand years ago. Similarly, we were expected to be able to come up with chapter and verse upon the presentation of the proper stimulus. Like Pavlov's dogs, we drooled dutifully.

After the grim fairy tales, we'll share an adventure in Aristotelian logic which should dismay and may even appall you. Then I shall whisk you back from the realm of Oberon and Titania into the garish light of day, and you will be strictly on your own. You may be somewhat annoyed when it is all over, but do you remember how you felt when you first discovered that Hans Christian Andersen had only been kidding, after all?

FAIRY TALE NUMBER ONE

The Fire-Breathing Dragon of Homogeneous Grouping

Once upon a time, and not so very long ago at that, it was the sacred duty of Education's loyal sons to fight to the death against any form of ability grouping which might raise its horrid head. Research projects spawned like rabbits, each proving beyond a doubt that taking smart kids away from their stupid classmates and educating them separately was undemocratic, reactionary, and generally pernicious. Besides, it was impossible. Everybody knew a few years ago that ability grouping never worked because children who were homogeneous in one respect were bound to be heterogeneous in all others, and so on and on, right down to the last standard deviation.

So what happens?

So Conant comes along and recommends homogeneous grouping. Suddenly we all find ourselves nodding and saying, "Of course. Common sense indicates that gifted kids are going to progress faster if the shackles are taken off."

We try the treasonable but reasonable suggestion, and behold! it works. Common sense, for a change, triumphs. Conant is right.

But where was all this common sense just five short years ago, hmmm?

FAIRY TALE NUMBER TWO

The Enchanted Maturation Level

When I was just a broth of a high-school principal, the Wise Men of the profession all told me that algebra should never, never be taught any earlier than the tenth grade because the older the child, the more easily he learned algebra. I had a fuzzy, uneasy feeling at the time that if I were to pursue this thesis to its logical conclusion I would end up offering algebra only to postgraduate students, but, like Scarlett O'Hara, I decided to think about that tomorrow.

Teaching a college-preparatory foreign language in junior high was looked upon as so outrageous a proposition that no one even dared to think about that at all.

Then there was kindergarten. The slightest hint of formal instruction in this preserve of nose blowing and toilet training caused every primary supervisor within a radius of five hundred miles to swarm to the attack like so many maddened barracuda. I almost hate to bring it up here, but recently certain institutions which shall remain discreetly nameless have actually been teaching kindergartners to *read*. Well! When I read *that* one, my head swam, my eyes lifted involuntarily to Heaven, and I waited numbly for the Second Coming.

But the world jogs on, and apparently the planet is going to muddle along for a few years to come, anyhow. In more and more schools next year, certain eighth-graders will be exposed to algebra, biology, and even Latin, and quite a few five-year-olds will be reading just as merrily as though what they are doing would not have constituted educational heresy when you and I were young, Maggie.

You ask what I'm doing about it?

Oh, just turning over some of the sizable rocks out this way to try and locate some of those experts who were so positive only the other day that it couldn't be done.

FAIRY TALE NUMBER THREE
The Ugly Ogre of Homework

Remember the doghouse inhabited by homework from 1945 to 1955?

It was busy work, remember? It was a dastardly incursion upon the sacred right of kids to loaf and raise hell after school. It was the last refuge of a poor teacher. And, inevitably, we had the usual crop of researchers who demonstrated triumphantly that children who did no homework accomplished just as much in school as those who burned the midnight oil.

So comes the Space Age, and all our most reputable authorities suddenly come out for at least fifteen hours per week for high-school pupils, and about an hour a day for the upper elementary grades. We implement this proposal like mad, and what do we find? Why, that the small fry are learning more, covering more ground, and notably failing to increase the population of the nation's rest homes, sanitariums, and other nut farms.

Now that we really think about it, it's reasonable that increased study time will produce increased mastery, isn't it?

So how come we didn't think this way back in 1955? I'm just asking.

FAIRY TALE NUMBER FOUR
The Giants and the Dwarfs

Many years ago, when I was trying to become a teacher and was still too young to recognize a liar when I heard one, my old professor used to tell me, "The content of the subject taught is of minimal importance. What is significant are the attitudes and values which rise out of the inter-relationship of the teacher and the pupils."

They actually believed this stuff, you know. *What* was taught was far less important than *how* it was taught. Trigonometry might be trivial, basket weaving basic. If the child learned more togetherness, more in-groupness, more forward-looking, on-going self-actualizing (I am quoting here, in case you were in any doubt, and you can supply the name of your favorite authority), why then he should continue in basket weaving, or cake decorating, or advanced locker opening, or whatever it was that was giving him this vital, rewarding experience. The fact that we were wildly wasting our country's precious resources of brains and talent by diluting them with pap didn't seem to register with us at all.

The Sputniks put an end to most of this guff, of course. It's a bold curriculum consultant who will come right out in public today and say that woodworking is as important as physics. He'll agree, now, with those of us who have been saying for quite a spell that America's survival depends upon the students of chemistry and calculus and languages rather than upon the worthy patrons of upholstering and badminton and second-year table-setting. He'll admit—now —that in the hierarchy of subject matter there are giants and there are dwarfs.

How did it happen, I wonder, that in the early 1950s they all looked the same size to him and to his ilk?

FAIRY TALE NUMBER FIVE
The Sleeping Princess Life Adjustment

Education as adjustment to one's environment is sleeping these days behind a prickly and impenetrable hedge of unpleasant statistics and facts of life, mostly furnished by our practical friends the Russians. But what a long and happy and thoroughly mischievous life our sleeping princess had before she went to sleep!

"All values are relative," she would intone sweetly. "All truths are mutable. All standards are variable. The only thing worth teaching, therefore, is the ability to react to an ever-shifting environmental kaleidoscope. Adjust. Adjust. Adjust."

And she would wave her magic wand, and a few more solids would fall out of the curriculum.

This, whether we like to admit it or not, was the educational philosophy of the 1930s, the 1940s, and most of the 1950s. Don't try to mold your environment; let it shape you. Don't try to stand out; fit in. Your goal was to belong, to conform, to be accepted. The Organization Man: this is what we worked so long and so hard to turn out. Masses of gray-flanneled oafs, agreeable, subservient, content—adjusted.

Where would Shelley have been in our schools, I wonder? What would have been the fate of Byron or Newton or Churchill, those gleaming gifted few who come along once or twice in a century to share with the great humdrum mass that is the rest of us the ambrosia of their genius?

We who called ourselves educators throughout this period had forgotten one of the great truths of Education —or perhaps it was never told to us: that the men who have moved mountains and worked wonders have not done so because they adjusted to their peer groups.

FAIRY TALE NUMBER SIX
The Transformed Educator

"If we can't find the answer, let's ask Teacher."

Not any more, kiddies. Not unless the answer is plainly written in the book, and even then Teacher might not be able to figure it out.

You see, Teacher doesn't read very well any more, children. He's not so hot at spelling, either. In history, he's very apt to confuse the Wars of the Roses with the Flowering of New England. And the geographical distinction between Guinea and Guiana leaves him hopelessly confused.

Nobody has made Teacher learn anything for a long, long time, boys and girls. Except about How To Teach, of course. Even here, he's a little backward. Because he comes from the Lower Level of the great university, little friends. Everyone there is smarter than he is.

But cheer up. He can always ask the Principal how to punctuate his unsatisfactory notices, can't he?

And if the Principal doesn't know, there's always the Superintendent. Isn't there?

This is the saddest fairy tale of all. . . .

FAIRY TALE NUMBER SEVEN
The Mythical Monster Merit Pay

The National Education Association and all its embattled subsidiaries have for the past ten years stood like King Arthur and his knights of the Round Table, swinging their battle-axes and hacking desperately away at the hydra-headed monster Merit Pay.

We have been regaled with horror stories about districts that tried it back in 1923 and have never fully recovered from the effects, of whole faculties whose collective virginity was so crassly violated that they resigned *en masse* rather than accept more money, of the impossibility of accurately rating a teacher unless at least the grandchildren of his present pupils have lived and died.

We have been told by regiments and squadrons of experts that merit pay turns teachers into Machiavellian connivers, or espionage agents *a la* Peter Lorre, or despondent mopers because their delicate sensibilities can't stand the shock of being compared to others of their kind.

Horsefeathers.

The truth, naturally enough, is that merit pay is being tried in many different forms in an increasing number of districts every year. It's working, too. In my own state, the number of districts under merit pay has doubled in one year.

This is one fairy tale that will probably be around a while. But not too much longer.

So there you have them, gentlemen—the Seven Grim Fairy Tales, myths made up out of the filmiest of cobwebs, the most fragile of gleaming bubbles, the most transient of dewdrops. Like all fairy stories, they are the stuff that dreams are made of. They differ from the legends of our childhood in that we have been conditioned to believe them. A generation of the American people has been brought up and nurtured on fairy tales. Against the faceless masses and the sinister science of the Asian steppes, we have armed our fellow countrymen with the brittle silver swords and the glistening hollow shields of Fairyland.

When we began this little journey beyond the frontiers of fantasy, I promised you an exercise in Aristotelian logic. Here it is for you to quarrel with, vulnerable perhaps from a strictly technical standpoint but attired nevertheless in impeccably syllogistic costume.

MAJOR PREMISE: For thirty years, our Columbia University philosophers, our educational psychologists, and our state department consultants have been leading us down a primrose path where report cards read like Abbott and Costello comedy routines, where competition was a naughty word, and where memorization and drill were relics of the Dark Ages. All the while, these same gentlemen kept assuring us that this was the way to the brave new world—to peace, to happy child development, to Adjustment.

Okay so far?

MINOR PREMISE: In the last three years, we have found out for ourselves that our morals are rotten, our world position degenerating so abysmally that a race of lash-driven atheistic peasants can challenge us successfully in our own chosen field of science, and our rate of juvenile murder, torture, rape, and perversion so much the highest in the world that it has become an object of shuddering horror to the rest of the human race. More, our greatest leaders today, both in and out of Education, now assure us that these fairy stories with which we have for thirty years bulwarked our thinking and our actions are just—plain—not—true.

And so we come to the inescapable

CONCLUSION: Ladies and gentlemen, we have been sold a bill of goods.

There is no alternative. Either we were wrong in 1935 and 1945 and 1955, or we are wrong now.

Either it is bad for children to have to do homework after school, or it isn't.

Either it is bad to separate certain pupils from their fellows and educate them apart, or it isn't.

Either it is bad to recognize that some subjects in school are of less importance than others, or it isn't.

Either it is bad to stress competition in school as preparation for the jungle that is twentieth-century life, or it isn't.

We are like Alice. We have stepped into the looking glass and found everything exactly the opposite from what we have always been led to believe.

How, then, do we know that we are right today? We know it for one eminently down-to-earth reason. We have been seized by the scruff of the neck and compelled by the fell clutch of circumstance to do what we are reluctantly and belatedly having to do. If we fail to do it, we will not survive. It's just as simple as that.

And if for a generation and more we have been conned into doing things that actually worked against our survival as a free nation, then just where does this leave the life-adjustment boys with the horn-rimmed spectacles and the group dynamics—the professors who wrote those long books in praise of "social living" and "fusion courses"— and the antique, thin-lipped spinsters of a hundred county offices and a score of state departments of education who sat at the feet of John Dewey a lifetime ago and, like the

Bourbons of old, have learned nothing and forgotten nothing through all the empty, weary years?

We all know what these characters are doing today, don't we?

They're feverishly writing more books and more articles showing how analytical geometry should be put back into the high-school curriculum along with four years of Russian, and advocating the teaching of laboratory science in the first grade. They're busy doing everything they can to make everyone forget that they ever told poor little wet-behind-the-ears student teachers to bake sourdough biscuits in order to teach sixth graders about Alaska, to construct mud huts in the middle of the classroom floor so that a unit on the Congo might be "sensorily demonstrated," and to build igloos out of Frigidaire ice cubes in order to appreciate the great cultural contributions of the Eskimos.

Isn't it about time we turned these folklore specialists out to pasture?

To save ourselves and our country, we are going to have to forget the fairy tales. We must emerge from the incense fumes and the murky smoke of the old myths and prepare to deal with reality. And we must set our steps, with those of the children whose lives have been entrusted to our care, upon the rocky but rewarding path of sweat and service and sacrifice. Nothing more than this is necessary. Nothing less will do.

After all, nothing is basically wrong with our profession which a little intelligence can't cure. And to date, that's just what we've got.

Damned little. . . .

► *One thing which the Pragmatists had always set much store by was the principle of Utilitarianism. A method or system was to be judged, they said, only in terms of its demonstrable outcomes. But when the People began to look and to lay about them in the cold, gray morn which followed Sputnik, they found to their horror that at least one of the Demonstrable Outcomes of the mating between permissive Progressivism and soulless Behaviorism had been a Monster. . . .*

The Cult of the Slob

5

*Is this the Thing the Lord God made and gave
To have dominion over sea and land . . . ?*

MARKHAM

WE SPEAK TODAY of changes—desirable or necessary—
in the high schools of the land. Ladies and gentlemen, I
invite you to consider with me the case of the triumphant
Slob. . . .

He stands before us at this moment, unwashed and un-
regenerate. His hair is agleam and adrip with oil, kneaded
behind into strange whorls and sinuosities. Below the ears
and following the slack jaw line, it descends in bristling
tufts, and with an exuberance unknown since the more
militant days of the late General Burnside. Hairiness, in
fact, is the very badge and symbol of the Slob. He spends
a considerable portion of his day coiling and matting, as
the Mock Turtle did reeling and writhing.

Our Slob is apt to wear his clothing much as the ladies
of Regency days flaunted their bodices—for purposes of
revealing rather than concealing. His shirt is open to the
fourth button, coyly baring naked flesh down even to the
navel. Trousers are slick denim, buckled low upon the hips
and hinting at an eager willingness to go even lower.
Boots are standard Slob attire, as is the cheap leather jacket
with GENTS or ROADRUNNERS blazoned luridly upon its back.

His stance approximates the so-called debutante slouch
of a generation ago. His walk is an exaggerated, hip-swing-

ing roll which harks back to the gait of the old salt-water sailor temporarily marooned on land. His talk is a modern thieves' jargon, relying strongly upon scarcely disguised obscenity and intelligible mainly to other members of the cult. His music is the monotonous and nerve-racking drumbeat of the primeval jungle.

If we were to overcome our instinctive revulsion long enough to institute a more intimate search of the Slob's person, we should find exotic treasure indeed. Aside from the miscellaneous and unprintable items of pornography which we may expect as a matter of course, we are bound to come upon several pieces of equipment which will cause even our experienced eyebrows to do a demivolt. I do not refer here to the ubiquitous switchblade knife, normally used to enforce terrorized quiescence upon the victim of a mass rape. Nor do I allude to the bicycle chain, commonly swung menacingly about the heads of smaller boys in order to collect protection money, nor even to the zip gun which lends a deadly note to the gang rumbles.

No, I have reference rather to the inked or tattooed device worn upon the hand or arm, strikingly suggestive of an unholy brotherhood of crime and startlingly reminiscent of the Maffia. I allude in passing also to such esoteric appurtenances as the razor-studded cap brim for slashing faces, and the shortened tire iron for breaking legs. Surely such a walking chamber of horrors should at least cause us to pause for consideration.

I am reminded in this connection of the Duke of Wellington's comment when confronted with a somewhat similar situation. During the Peninsular Campaign, the Duke kept the sea lanes to London sizzling with his insistent demands for reinforcements. After an interminable delay, the laggard troops arrived in Spain, but to everyone's horror, they turned out to be jailbirds and sturdy rogues, the scourings of the London streets. As the Iron Duke sat glumly on his horse before the heights of Torres Vedras watching the clumsy recruits attempting to drill, an eager aide approached him.

"Tell me, m'Lord, d'ye think these blighters will frighten old Boney?"

The Duke regarded him grimly.

"I can't say about Boney, but by God they frighten *me!*"

I must confess that I am with the Duke in this matter. They frighten *me*.

It is these added refinements, these supererogatory icings on the cake of delinquency which in my opinion constitute ample cause for our serious study of the Slob in any symposium on high-school problems. In sober truth, and especially since educators have of late become prime targets of the Slob's more lethal aggressions, we are left with little choice other than to initiate an examination of Slobbism, if only out of self-defense.

After all, so long as the characters who lurched menacingly about our high-school corridors and snarled defiantly at their teachers confined their activities to mere lurching and snarling, it was expedient for us to chalk up such behavior to "release of tensions" and "animal spirits" and to let it go at that. A good many of our abler instructors, it is true, dropped out of the business, unable or unwilling to assume the role of Frank Buck constantly challenging the carnivores, and some of the hardier souls who stuck it out were carried out feet first as the result of brushes with certain of their pupils whose tensions they had unwittingly helped to release. But minor blood-letting such as this was dismissed by school administrators as statistically inconsequential, and life in the Great American High School rocked and rolled along its accustomed path.

Until recently . . .

When, a few months ago, a junior-grade disciple of Slobbism toted his rifle to school for kicks, and spent the better part of a half-hour chivvying his startled principal from office to lavatory as the hot lead flew.

And a short time later, another junior-high principal was so bedeviled and humiliated and just plain scared that he chose to solve his problems by jumping off a roof and spattering himself all over a playground, while the Slobs stood by and sniggered.

Then, more recently, the crash of shotgun fire added a touch of piquancy to the run-of-the-mill noises of a California campus as a sulky Slob blew the leg off an athletic director who had been unwise enough to intervene between the grinning gunman and a potential victim.

It may seem at first glance that these examples of Slobbism are excessively sanguinary, but simple assault and battery in the schools is, quite frankly, too common to talk about. Almost every edition of your favorite newspaper contains a matter-of-fact story about some schoolman who has been slugged or roughed up by a pack of punks. Such treatment is coming to be regarded as just another occupational hazard, ranking somewhere on the scale between simple writer's cramp and accumulation of chalk dust in the lungs. So long as this one-sided tong war took place outside the inner sanctum of the principal or the superintendent, we administrators were inclined to shrug it off.

Isolated instances, you know. . . .

Or, "Mr. Jones brought it on himself, in a way. Had trouble establishing rapport."

But recent happenings have placed things in a somewhat different light. The zip-gun sights have been raised, and Mr. Administrator is finding himself uncomfortably in dead center. His concern has ceased to be academic, and is rapidly becoming personal. I can only assume that a good many of my colleagues, in the face of imminent stabbing or shooting, are going to revise their priority listings of significant high-school problems to place Slobbism somewhere up near the top.

At least, they will if they are as downright cowardly as I am.

Even if schoolmen turn out to be heroes, however, it is still high time to concern ourselves with the peculiar problem posed by this twentieth-century version of *homo neanderthalensis*. A school is neither a battleground nor a hunting preserve, and unless we address ourselves energetically to the solving of this puzzle, we are going to find ourselves increasingly beset within our ivory towers by baying bands of Slobs. So perhaps the mills of the gods, by grinding perilously near our persons, may compel us at last to take the action which the scandalous and pitiful plight of our normal, decent pupils, terrorized by these creeps, has so long demanded of us.

The old head-in-the-sand technique of minimizing or ignoring the size of the Slob in the hope that he will somehow get lost won't work any more. It has been fashionable to say smugly that these are maladjusted boys, thrown up through no fault of their own from the modern maelstrom of wars, depressions, and broken homes. To this pious platitude is usually appended the magnificent *non sequitur* that, after all, these social deviates compose but a very small fraction of the total adolescent population. A similar observation, of course, might be made with equal truth about the cholera bacillus.

It is important that we understand our enemy. And it is an enemy we are talking about, not just a misunderstood by-product of the machine age. The Slob, or more importantly the whole institution of Slobbism, is the mortal adversary of Education.

Slobbism negates all the values that we teach.

It convulses hysterically against all disciplines.

It derides morality in any form.

It persistently seeks out ugliness and filth in preference to beauty and decency, like the unlovely but irreproachably Biblical dog which insisted on returning to its vomit.

Above all, it takes pleasure in inflicting pain.

The Slob is thus the exact opposite of the gentleman, who is defined by Newman as one who never willingly inflicts pain. Our Slob not only inflicts pain; he revels in it. The threatening note, the obscene phone call, the ravaging of women and children—these are the Slob's stock in trade. Indeed, it has been truly said that his sole interests are sadism, sex, and speed, in that order.

The Slob's mental processes are so rudimentary as to be almost nonexistent, although a certain amount of animal cunning is sometimes to be found in his agile twisting and turning to avoid work and to remain out of jail. The brain, however, is not so much deficient as unused. It has been short-circuited by a constant succession of appeals to the emotions. The Slob is ruled by his passions. He warms easily to rage. He burns with lust upon the slightest pretext. He shivers, occasionally, with clammy fear. He is adrenal rather than cerebral, physical rather than mental.

He is, in short, the perfect antithesis of everything Education stands for. The paradox lies in the fact that he is also the product of Education. A dozen years ago, he was in our kindergarten. He went on our field trips to the bakery, and danced around ribboned poles at our May festivals. Only yesterday, he was studying "social living" in our junior highs. He has been tested and guided and motivated. It has cost the taxpayers, over a decade or so, several thousand dollars to produce a Slob. It hardly seems worth it, does it?

Is there any hope of brightening this gloomy picture?

First, let us clear the ground by conceding in advance some of the more obvious truisms. Let us concede that the great majority of our high-school children are as yet free from the grosser manifestations of Slobbism. We can agree, too, on the essentially nonschool origins of the phenomenon. But when all this has been said, it does not follow that Education is absolved of all responsibility for the golems who stalk its halls.

Whose fault is it that no more exciting and rewarding goal than sheer sensuality has succeeded in capturing the imagination of these people? Hedonism, after all, is as old as the hills. Its lure was exploded before Christ. Surely Education can, if it tries, break in upon the sterile, revolving-door cycle of liquor and licentiousness.

Who is to blame for the pathological inability of these persons to concentrate for more than a few fleeting moments on anything less basic than feeding, fighting, and fornicating? Could it possibly stem from the chaotic mish-mash of canal building, Hopi Indians, tomato growing, air transport, and steel puddling through which we have merry-go-rounded our pupils in recent years? Is it possible that we have produced a group unamenable to discipline simply because we have never insisted upon their mastering anything which required discipline to overcome?

It is barely conceivable that, by destroying the hierarchy of values which placed mastery of specific subject matter in a position of paramount importance, we have persuaded these already confused minds that nothing in life, including life itself, is of any particular importance. We have re-quired them to go to school, but we have not required them to do any work. Instead we have created special "courses" wherein they might sprawl and leer in company with one another, and where constructive learning is laughed out of court. To the Slob, life is a dirty joke, with school the cream of the jest and educators the buffoons.

One way or another, the Slob must go. Those of his ilk who have passed the point of no return must be excluded from our schools as socially uneducable, even as we exclude the unfortunate imbecile as mentally uneducable. And let no one challenge our right to take this step. The Slob is more dangerous to his classmates than a walking case of typhoid or tuberculosis. We have not only the right but the clear and positive duty to quarantine him. It is our shame that we have not done so sooner. What will become of him? When he has reached this stage, he has passed beyond our power to correct. He is no longer susceptible to Education. He has become a subject for criminology.

As Dr. Johnson said of the Scotsman, much may be done with the Slob if he be caught young enough. With a program of specific goals, scientific testing, understanding guidance, and consistent discipline, a school should be able to nip a great deal of Slobbism in the bud. If the school is fortunate enough to be located in a community where the police are alert, the courts tough, and the citizenry concerned, the cult of the Slob can be broken by the united action of all. Where such a happy combination of attitudes is not present, it becomes the positive duty of the school administration to work diligently within the community to produce it.

We have gone overboard on universal education. It has become a fetish instead of a logically considered objective. By our stubborn refusal to exclude clearly pathological cases from school, we are presently permitting this fetishism to work irremediable wrong upon the great majority of normal children whom we are exposing to this moral plague. It is my conviction that Slobbism is a highly contagious disease. It must be treated as such. Isolation and prophylaxis are strongly indicated.

Law cannot help the deliberate homicide. He defies it.

Medicine cannot help the would-be suicide. He rejects it.

Religion cannot help the hardened atheist. He disbelieves it.

Even so, Education cannot help the full-blown Slob. He loathes it.

It is a sorry tribute to our perspicacity as schoolmen that we have let this thing drift to the point where many of us have become quivering quarry in our own classrooms. I submit that it will be pointless and tragic folly for us and for our country if we stand dithering by while the throat of Education is slowly cut with a switchblade knife.

▶ *Then, too, there were the Outcomes at the other end of the scale. These were not in the Monster category—far from it. But they were certainly different. And since conformity and adjustment and benign blending were the very warp and woof of the Pragmatic philosophy, no one for a very long time knew quite what to do with these little Outcomes who were so different, and who looked at the world around them with eyes so much clearer and wiser and—alas! —too often sadder than ours. . . .*

Esau's Children

6

WILL YOU JOIN me in a nightmare?

You find yourself in a strange, misshapen city. You walk bemused in the ragged shadows of marred buildings, aborted seemingly from the drawing boards of idiot architects. Everything seems raw and incomplete. The colors of the signs and blinking lights are not quite true; garish and lurid, they leap painfully against the eye. Common objects of daily use seem oddly lumpish and unfinished. Everywhere are signs of chaos and unreason. It is as though a vast flaw exists, palpable but elusively out of focus in the whole fabric of man's handiwork.

Nightmare Town has no dearth of pulsing machines and humming engines, but the ends they serve seem meaningless and puerile. Newspapers are hawked harshly, but the events they chronicle are tawdry and unreal. The books of Nightmare Town are childish primers. Its art is junk. Its music assaults the ear. Its politics equate with its crime, and both glare sullenly with the red eyes of the ancestral ape from the littered alleys and murky backrooms of the city. Every aspect repels, and yet mingled inextricably with the revulsion thus evoked are faint, sad glimmers of nobility, hints of lost fineness, tragic glimpses of some far-off might-have-been.

Naked, Nightmare Town is merely pathetic. Clothed with its citizenry, it becomes a city out of Hell.

The denizens of your dream are multitudinous. They throng the roaring streets in their thousands, and lap fitfully about the skirts of the misshapen buildings. You approach them eagerly, questioning first one, then another, in the hope that among the swarming forms may lie the answer to your questions.

The hope dies hard.

Responses come easily, but the words mean little. Rambling and fragmentary, they hint at much but come to nothing. There seems scant meaning in the flowing syllables, though the curious crowd that rings you nods and gestures meaningfully at each word. As you stride desperately from one smiling chatterer to another, the nods behind your back become more scornful; the gestures become mocking finger taps against bobbing foreheads. You stop short. As you look with enforced calm for some glimmer of comprehension in the vacant faces, a sharp suspicion stabs deep. Your search becomes more specific, seeking now for certain stigmata which you know so well and dread so much to find.

Your fears are just. The signs are there. Each resident of the city wears them as he would a badge—the empty eyes, the vacuous smile, the untied shoes, the occasional drool. The truth rolls in upon you. Nowhere in this land is there a kindred soul to yours. Should one by chance exist, he is submerged beyond hope of discovery in the vast population pool. You are cut off from your kind. Worse still, you have no way of knowing in this strange world that you are not unique. Your kind may not even exist.

You are alone.

The inhabitants of your nightmare are imbeciles to a man.

The plans you dared to make will die unborn. No one could possibly understand them.

The goals you envision so proudly are meaningless in this society. Your love for order and logic and reason is destined to batter fruitlessly against the iron gates of stupidity. You are a hopeless minority of one, and will suffer the usual fate of minorities, without the solace of friend or follower. Even the fiery comfort of martyrdom will be denied you. In this world, there will be no one to appreciate or comprehend a martyr.

Here it will be best for you to wake up. Since the human mind is not constructed to contemplate infinite isolation with impunity, you will awaken, mop your brow, and shakily profane the Welsh rarebit you had for supper.

But suppose you could not wake up.

If you are one in a hundred million, one out of a score or so born each generation, you will not wake up. You are already awake. You are doomed to live out your life immersed in a sea of humanity as alien to you in ability and understanding as lead is inferior to fine gold. You are condemned to long years of such intellectual loneliness as it is difficult for the average mind to imagine. Mentally, you are well-nigh unique.

You see, you are a genius.

And the rest of us scurry blindly around you, gently drooling. . . .

The nightmare sketched above is stark reality for a microscopically small percentage of mankind. It is most real for the true genius, whose IQ of 175–200 places him as far above those of us who boast normality as we find ourselves above the imbecile. It is equally real, though to a somewhat lesser degree, in the case of the gifted, who may be only 50 or 60 points above us on the mental scale. To these somewhat more numerous individuals, we are in a category analogous to that which the low-grade moron occupies in relation to ourselves.

Under the circumstances, it is small wonder that the mortality rate among the world's geniuses has been traditionally high. During the authoritarian Middle Ages, many of them must have perished at the stake, even as their modern counterparts died out in Germany under the brief regime of the unspeakable Hitler. America has treated its few geniuses with irregular affection. Steinmetz and Mark Twain were showered with honors; Hawthorne and Emily Dickinson barricaded themselves from public cruelty in furtive isolation; Poe insulated his hypersensitivity with alcohol and laudanum. Some have quietly starved; others have beaten their priceless brains out against the walls of madhouse cells.

Almost never has one of these tormented titans taken his revenge against the society which rejected him by declaring war against it and devoting his terrifying talents to the destruction of humanity. Terman has told us that the so-called military geniuses like Napoleon and Genghis Khan were really men of only slightly above average intellect. By the grace of a singularly kind Providence, it has apparently been decreed that the higher the intelligence, the greater the aversion to violence. The "criminal genius" in the true sense of the term does not exist. For this seemingly built-in safety factor, humanity may well be thankful.

By the same token, however, blind violence seems to haunt the ultraviolet levels of the intelligence spectrum. As we descend the ladder into the several moron strata, we find a proportionate rise in violent attitudes and actions. The genius thus finds himself doubly at a disadvantage; he is often the object of persecution by a violent majority against whom his basic aversion to violence forbids him to defend himself. Fortunately for his chances of personal survival but unfortunately for the advancement of mankind, his intellect dictates a definite and unmistakable course which will not only enable him to pass relatively unnoticed in a "normal" world, but will also afford some brief snatches of happiness. This device, when found among the lower animals, we call protective coloration. The subject blends indistinguishably into the landscape. As adapted by the genius, the technique calls for him to imitate deliberately the "normality" of his family, schoolfellows, or business associates. He purposely suppresses his great gift that he may live at peace with his neighbors. All of us in the education profession have watched this technique operate in our classrooms as the myriad weapons of the mass mind play destructively upon the sensitive intellects of the lonely gifted.

The results, from the standpoint of society, are nothing short of catastrophic. Recent statistics indicate that half our gifted young people never enter college. They have come to terms with a world which puts a glittering premium upon the essentially nonintellectual activities of the business world and attaches stern penalties to the once-prized fields of art, poetry, and music. Even science no longer challenges their best, since great areas of science are now devoted to wholesale destruction. They find themselves in a world culture which is prepared to accept them only upon its own terms, never upon theirs. What we are witnessing, then, is mass abdication of the gifted. In the same manner that the light-skinned Negro "passes" as white, and with the same motives, the gifted are "passing" as normal. Their achievements, sadly but inevitably, are normal, also.

Our profession has traditionally dealt with the problem of the gifted in two ways: acceleration and enrichment. Neither has worked, but the second is less corrosive than the first.

Acceleration is the easy way out. The teacher finds herself somewhat embarrassed by the bright-eyed fifth grader who can spell infinitely better than she can, and who knows that Tananarive is the capital of Madagascar at a time when his fellow students are having trouble locating the continent of Africa. The teacher feels inferior, and no wonder. Intellectually, the "bright one" bears the same relation to her that she bears to the lowest member of her class. So she tells her principal that Eddie is not being "challenged," and urges that he be placed with his intellectual peers.

This is, of course, ridiculous. In the school—nay, in the whole city—Eddie may not have an intellectual peer. What the teacher means is that Eddie should be placed on the instructional level corresponding to his latest achievement rating. This may be the seventh or even eighth grade, and has the quintessential advantage of getting Eddie not only out of the fifth grade but also out of the entire elementary school. So Eddie goes to junior high school at the age of ten and does well scholastically, as indeed he probably would have done had they sent him to Cal Tech.

The unequal contest between Eddie and Society has now begun. It does not take long for the stripes and buffets to rain down.

Eddie is now the Class Freak.

He is too small for the games and sports which bulk so large in early adolescence. He is too young for the parties and dances that celebrate the first stirrings of sex, a phenomenon which Eddie with all his brains is hardly in a position to evaluate properly. As far as his instructors are concerned, Eddie becomes a sort of human yardstick against which all scholastic standards are automatically measured. Moreover, he is young, small, and therefore "cute." What more devastating concatenation of circumstances can be imagined than to be regarded on the one hand by his class-mates either patronizingly as an oddity or coldly as a "brain" and on the other hand by his teachers as a pet or a paragon?

College, unless Eddie rebels first and becomes a street-car conductor, merely confirms the damage done by ac-celeration. He enters the ivied halls at the age of fifteen, and promptly finds all doors closed to him except the one leading to scholastic achievement.

Fraternities? "We're not pledging babies, thank you."

Football? "Want the kid to get killed?"

Dances? "My dear, guess who asked me to the prom. Why, that little Eddie Smith boy. I think he's just as cute as he can be, and everyone says he's just awfully smart, but my dear, he makes me feel like an old lady."

Campus politics? "We're not after the junior high vote these days, bud."

So Eddie becomes a grind and a bookworm, or worse. The road to maladjustment lies open before him, with the other avenues to status and success all barricaded and hung with detour signs. The gifts which God intended him to share with his fellows are stifled in gestation. The golden years of youth, that bank balance upon which all of us should be able to draw in memory during those later years when the blood runs thin and the joy of living ebbs, are wincing, painful years for Eddie, years of rejection, tacit or explicit. Not for him will come the slippered, firelit hours of happy reverie, the conjuring up of thronging visions of joyous faces and youthful voices. College memories for Eddie will be those of grim and humdrum routine, a thing to be buried, not treasured in remembrance.

A man defrauded of his inheritance is apt to be bitter, to suspect his friends, to murmur silently against the existing order of things. Such a man will Eddie be in the normal course of events. Such, no doubt, were the children of Esau, when they saw their birthright traded for a mess of pottage.

So much for acceleration.

Enrichment offers greater promise, but too often fails to live up to the expectations of its advocates. Theoretically, it should be possible to permit a fifth grader to remain in the fifth grade, no matter how gifted he may be. He can do research; he can perform experiments; he can write creatively. His gifts of leadership can flower in the gentle sunshine of his own age group. Book reports and biographical sketches should flow from his pen. His murals and cartoons should decorate the room. The playground and the library alike should serve as arenas for the exuberance of his swift-flowing talents.

But all this is theory.

Faced with forty-pupil classes, double sessions, and un-trained teachers, theory breaks down in a hurry. The whole school organism, grappling with the mushrooming child mass as a python strives to ingest an outsize calf, writhes and thrashes. The gifted child is squeezed into conformity by the undulating coils or swallowed whole. Today's schools operate on a bare survival level; what have they to do with the cultivation of the rare and the exotic? Enrichment for the gifted finds itself today in the precise position of the ancient idol whose worshipers genuflected and paid lip service, but from whose altar the sacrificial meats were surreptitiously filched.

If acceleration and enrichment are alike blind alleys, where are we to look for the right answers?

Segregation of the gifted? Perhaps. Yet this runs counter to most sound educational doctrine, and meets with a formidable opponent in our American concept of demo-cratic equality. Whatever solution we adopt must find its roots in our native ideals and beliefs; even our prejudices can by no means be ignored. The problem is as old as Plato, but, unlike that genial philosopher, we must be sure that our solution does not remain forever untried, embalmed between the covers of a book, no matter how immortal.

If special opportunity for the gifted is un-American, so is every college football team. So is our Olympic track and field squad. So is the college preparatory course in every high school of the nation, and the entrance requirements of the universities themselves. So long as education of the gifted is not restricted to any system of economic or racial group, so long as it is free to all who can qualify, it is as eminently defensible as training for the retarded, which few question and which is organized on exactly the same principle. Democracy does not consist in putting every boy in school on the track team; it *does* consist in giving every boy an opportunity to try out for it.

Let us assume in our approach that some degree of segregation will be needed if the gifted are to be helped. Let us also agree that a combination of several educational techniques will probably be needed to meet the requirements of so precocious and specialized a group. Finally, let us proceed to set up a program designed primarily to identify and develop leadership from among the individuals in our society best fitted to lead—the gifted.

Here, then, is a suggested solution to the increasing problem of the genius and his kind.

1. *Find them.* How many "mute, inglorious Miltons" must there be whose abilities are never known, whose talents are never recognized? Every elementary and high-school pupil should receive regular intelligence testing at stated intervals, and every IQ rating above 140 subjected to the acid test of the Binet.

2. *Keep them with their age groups.* Rejecting the principle of acceleration, let us keep the gifted with children of their own age throughout the period of formal education.

3. *Enrich the primary grades.* We should develop testing devices of sufficient sensitivity to enable us to identify giftedness in the first grade, and then move Heaven and earth to provide maximum enrichment opportunities through the third grade.

4. *Segregate them four months each year.* Build great leadership schools in every state. From the fourth grade on, make it possible for all gifted children to attend these schools free of charge for four months each year. The leadership schools should be staffed with the top teachers of each state, and equipped with the finest educational tools that money can buy. Only the gifted would be eligible to attend, and they would be exposed to every intellectual stimulus which the ingenuity of psychology and the resources of modern Education can devise. Attendance at these schools would be entirely voluntary, but parents of the gifted should be informed fully about the advantages accruing from such attendance.

5. *Place them in specially chosen homes.* The children should be placed in private homes carefully screened for cultural and intellectual excellence. Families surviving such a screening should be approached and interested in offering temporary homes for gifted children from other communities. Methods of selection may follow the pattern presently in effect for placing foreign exchange students. Children attending leadership schools would thus be assured of twenty-four-hour stimulus to the optimum degree. All expenses would be borne by the state.

5. *Return them periodically to their own communities.* During the balance of the year, the gifted children should be encouraged to live a normal and happy life with their own families, attending the schools of their home communities, and associating freely with the rank and file of humanity. After all, they will hardly be able to spend their later lives associating only with their own kind.

Such a program is open to criticism, but it has the merit

of proposing steps which could almost immediately be put into effect. If any state is attempting seriously to help the gifted, it can hardly provide less than the financial equivalent of the program outlined above. The plan maintains good family relationships, childhood friendships, age groups, and local schooling. In addition and for a substantial portion of each year, the gifted child will be exposed to brilliant instruction, magnificent equipment, and the finest possible home environment. To have validity, any criticism of this program must provide the equivalent of all these features in a better form.

The world of tomorrow will be a fearful and wonderful place. The safest and most prudent course which we can follow now is to be sure that its destinies are placed in the hands of those best fitted to guide them.

Homo sapiens has a unique opportunity to guide into the future its own evolutionary pattern. It cannot afford to ignore its lonely advance guard in planning for the next great leap ahead in natural selection. In a very real sense, *Homo superior* may even now be waiting on our threshold.

► *Many of the results of the Progressive Blight were plainly visible to all who had eyes to see. Some, however, were subtly hidden, almost defying detection in the manner of a deficiency disease. For example, in the well-fed, overstuffed America of the 1950s, who would have thought to look for Famine? Yet Famine there was, though not of the granary or the packing house. The fact was that for some reason we were running in very short supply of a rare and irreplaceable commodity—Genius.*

How Doth the Little Busy Bee ... ? 7

IN ANY CONSIDERATION of the shape of things to come, there is one certainty which can be isolated, labeled, and nailed down, and that is this: it is not going to be fashioned after our own image. The forces acting upon us today are going to produce a world whose social structure will differ as greatly from our own as ours does from that of the anthropoid apes.

I have often felt that the most logical chauffeur for the late H. G. Wells to have placed in charge of his time machine for a jaunt into the future was not a physicist but an entomologist. Only an authority on insect life will feel at home in the strangely geometrical world order which will characterize the days beyond tomorrow. Especially would this sense of nostalgic familiarity become acute if our time traveler had previously specialized in bees or ants. Logic, you see, operates equally well on insects as on men, and often with similar results. The future may indeed hold for our descendants the City of God, as Augustine promised, but it will be in the image of the beehive. Or the anthill.

Since our tase for honey usually exceeds our tolerance for formic acid, let us examine for a moment the implications of an apiarian world.

A beehive is a comfortable place. It is warm, safe, and stocked with delicious food. Its inhabitants are disciplined, cooperative, and seemingly happy. They labor unceasingly in highly specialized but relatively pleasant jobs for the greater good of the hive. In return, they are cared for by the welfare state from the cradle to the grave, or rather from egg to bird's craw, to keep our parallels properly biological. They are perfectly adjusted to their environment. They are born, they eat, they reproduce, they die. It is difficult for the observer to detect any significant variations of conduct on the part of individual bees.

Such is the life of the social insect, and such it has been, unvarying and immutable, for fifty million years. One fault might perhaps be particularized by the carping critic, and since there will probably be no critics around in a few generations this may seem so negligible as to be scarcely worth considering. This dubious disadvantage is the previously mentioned liquidation of the individual.

Any bee larva which, touched and transmuted by some random cosmic ray, showed the faintest signs of becoming an apian Moses, Newton, or Leonardo da Vinci would ring alarm bells all over the hive and alert the aroused guardians of the elaborate structure to perform immediately the insect equivalent of euthanasia upon the unfortunate mutation. In justice to our ancient friends the bees, it should be pointed out that they would take equally drastic preventive action against any larval Hitlers, Stalins, or Genghis Khans.

They have thus achieved the delicate balance sought for compulsively by all advanced cultures. It is a subtle and highly developed society, operating for the good of all.

It is completely materialistic, absolutely egalitarian, and one hundred percent deadly to the atypical individual. It has found, apparently, that the individual is more trouble than he is worth, especially when vast population masses have to be provided for.

I submit that the bees, who are our senior citizens on this planet and who anticipate us by a good many millions of years, have arrived at this evidently final stage of their development through the pressure of ineluctable evolutionary forces acting upon uncounted billions of individuals. It is my further contention that similar forces acting upon the proliferating hordes of our own species will tend to produce similar results. For good measure and for what it may be worth, I will throw in the demonstrable theory that today's educators are helping the forces of evolution along to the very best of their ability.

Right about here, I can imagine the collective sniff exhaled from thousands of pedagogical nostrils: "What rot! My pupils may resemble a good many things, but busy little bees . . . ha!"

In rebuttal, had I the time, it could be pointed out that there are such things as drones, of which our own race, as well as that of our winged friends, has always had more than its share. But I prefer to confine my efforts to pointing out the trends of modern educational and cultural evolution, and to showing the inescapable parallel between what is happening to us and what has already happened to the higher insects.

The great dogma of Group Adaptation forms the cornerstone of twentieth-century educational theory. As laid down by the pragmatic philosophers who, paradoxically enough, professed to abhor all dogma, the only eternal verity is that of constant change and flux.

All values are relative.

All truths are mutable.

All standards are variable.

Therefore, the only thing really worth teaching to young people, as we said before, is the ability to react to an ever-shifting environmental kaleidoscope. It is the philosophy of the man on the roller coaster.

The goal of all this is adjustment. Whether we realize it or not, the aim of modern Education as it has been enunciated by its prophets and soothsayers is maximum adjustment to a fluctuating environment. To considerable degree, this objective is in the process of being attained. *Life* magazine a few years back referred to the current generation of collegians as "the best adjusted, least troublesome" yet. It also had some less complimentary things to say:

"They seem to be most comfortable in groups, and even tend to make dates by fours and sixes. They show no strong urge to glorify or to rebel against their surroundings. They are without public heroes or villains. They are reported to be not so wild as their parents, nor so hard working. They gripe less and hope less. They are willing homemakers and fall quickly into monogamy, more from imitation than from any moral or economic imperative. They are refreshingly free of bigotry or race prejudice; and they believe, if in anything, in democracy and the brotherhood of man. Yet they seem sceptical and incurious about the machinery and safeguards of democracy."

They have been educated to conform.

They have been conditioned to cooperate.

They have been trained to adjust.

In another generation or two, they should be ready for the hive.

Life's statement, of course, does not apply to the deviate delinquent, but it is certainly descriptive of the great majority. It is true, I suppose, that these young people will lead more comfortable lives than their parents, that as they come into more nearly perfect conformity with their surroundings they will tend to develop fewer neuroses, and that it will prove increasingly difficult for anyone to goad them into mutiny or revolution. All these things may be taken as positive gains. But are there no counterbalancing losses?

What ever happened to that great American renaissance of painting and sculpture and music which European observers so confidently predicted for this century when they visited this country in the early days of the republic? "Surely," one of them said enthusiastically, "a land so vast and fruitful, a people so ingenious and virile, composed of the best of all the nations of the earth, above all a nation so free, will put to shame the cultural achievements of past civilizations, and will, within another century, produce such masterpieces in the arts as will dwarf into insignificance the outpouring of classical culture."

It was reasonable. It was logical. It just didn't happen.

What did happen was the incredibly rapid growth of a civilization based upon swift communication and dedicated to creature comforts, but virtually sterile insofar as the production of artistic masterpieces was concerned. The American people had more reason to be happy than any nation that had gone before. They enjoyed life; indeed, they lived largely with that goal alone in view.

But most great contributions to the world's store of culture have been wrung like drops of blood from conflict and revolt.

Michelangelo was disfigured and bitter.

Poe was an alcoholic.

Byron was a cripple and a libertine.

Coleridge took dope.

Shelley was an atheist.

Beethoven was deaf, friendless, and a boor.

The parade goes on indefinitely. Poor, twisted lives and tragic deaths. Yet from these lives came immeasurable beauty, bequeathed as a rich legacy unto the race of men.

Today, society would shoulder the problems of these men and accept as a challenge the easing of their tensions.

Michelangelo would be sent to a plastic surgeon.

Poe would join Alcoholics Anonymous.

Byron would be buttonholed by marriage counselors.

Coleridge would undergo withdrawal treatments.

Shelley would be welcomed with open arms into any one of countless societies of freethinkers.

Beethoven would be fitted with a hearing aid.

Everything necessary would be done to bring them into optimum adjustment with the world about them. In the world of the future, it will be as unthinkable for a child to reach adulthood in a state of basic and unrelieved conflict as it will be for him to do so with a cleft palate.

We must not be too surprised, however, to discover that as we straighten Michelangelo's crooked nose and teach him how to win friends and influence people, we also eliminate future Sistine Chapels. A Shelley attuned perfectly to his environment might not envy the wild freedom of the skylark sufficiently to write immortal odes to the little wanderer of the skies. A sober and tranquil Poe may have small occasion to explore with morbid intensity the unutterable horrors which lie behind the mask of the Red Death. Let us eschew all beard tuggings and eyebrow raisings when we find that between the rising curve of universal adjustment and the falling curve of individual genius there is a perfect correlation.

After all, we can't have everything, can we?

But let us assume that we are not completely satisfied with our short journey into the yet-to-be, that we yearn after some way for us to have our cake and eat it too. There may be a way, but it will be a rocky and tortuous one, picking its path among the brambles of contrary statistics. What can a teacher do in the face of the twenty million dots which are being added annually to the world population map? How can an educator prevent worldwide psychiatry from adjusting us all into a universal mediocrity?

We can do this one thing, and may God and our children's children forgive us if we do not. We can remember that genius, little as we understand it, is beyond all cavil a phenomenon of the individual. Where the person of the individual has been held sacred, genius has thrived; where the individual has been throttled and ridiculed and debased, genius has fled. The Russian steppes, which once flowered with the golden magic of Tolstoi and Tchaikovsky, now shiver in the barren weeds of an occasional

Ehrenberg. This is no coincidence. The Russians have tried to cultivate group genius, and there is no such thing as group genius.

We can remember that a genius is essentially a nonconformist. He is sent among us to protest, to upset, to prod, and to shame us. He is not a comfortable person to have around, but he is far indeed from being a Communist, that archconformist of the modern world. He has other values and higher goals than we, but it is through genius that the race moves, once or twice in a century, on seven-league boots.

We can rediscover what seems to be a forgotten truth: that the men who made the earth move in new orbits, who have lifted humanity out of ruts and given it wings, have not adjusted to environment. They have adjusted environment to themselves. Impelled seemingly by some force outside themselves, these men, like novas in the summer heavens, burn themselves out in brief exuberance, but change the shape of constellations overnight. Let us not insist upon conformity.

And, above all, let us not surrender to the sheer weight of numbers. Because mankind is breeding in a veritable explosion of population, let us not numbly await the certainty of a Malthusian twilight of the gods. It may well be that the great contribution which America has yet to make in its cycle of universal history is the solution to this crucial problem—the survival of the individual in a world of multiplying billions. Surely in the hammering out of a mighty issue such as this there is a vital and unique role for Education to play, a role which each of us professing this great calling must act out and add to until the time comes for us to leave the stage to those who will come after us.

For tomorrow will come, in one way or another. Make no mistake. It is up to us, as educators, to determine whether in the onsurging and billowing wave of the future, mankind will hear the laughter and the shouting of free men, or the murmuring of innumerable bees.

▶ *Just in passing, it should be noted that some of the strange and almost eerie doings of the Education profession during these years were psychologically predictable and even inevitable, given the set of circumstances under which educators were forced to labor. Some of these, it is true, are part and parcel of Education in any time and clime. Some were highly unnecessary.*

Bangles, Baubles and Beads

8

PYTHAGORAS, OR ONE of his more mystically minded followers, taught that a man's life experience, to be complete, must embrace both Alpha and Omega—the beginning and the end. The idea was that before anyone could savor the fullness of life he must first gain the vital concept of totality. He must be able to perceive the inner meaning of things, to see how the individual entity proceeds inevitably from first causes and progresses majestically to the final conclusion. Only after experiencing such knowledge could a man find peace and fulfillment.

Now this philosophy would get about as short shrift in modern America as General Sherman before a jury of Georgians, but it seems to me that we educators should think about it a little. For quite a spell now we have been labeled the most frustrated of all the professions, and it may well be that somewhere in the above paragraph lies the reason for the charge.

Let's look at engineering. The able practitioner of this mathematical art is present at the conception, birth, and ultimate apotheosis in steel and concrete of his brain children. He enjoys Alpha and Omega not once in his lifetime but many times. His sense of completeness, of fulfillment, is ever present.

The ministry? The classic case of the Vicar of Wakefield, who presided over the births, christenings, marriages, and funerals of his humble parishioners, and who had time left over to pursue the seducer of his fair daughter over half of England, comes immediately to mind. Surely the good Vicar's vocational subject matter, his life-work material, contained the ingredient of completeness. The conclusions may not always have been satisfactory, but at least he got to see them.

In medicine and in law, the origins of the problems do not begin with the practitioner, but they are made clear to him as he studies the cases. The climax and termination of each case find the professional man present and functioning, for good or ill. He perceives completion. He experiences fulfillment.

What of Education?

It has long been a puzzle to me that no one has ever put his finger on the one factor which more than any other stands out to make Education unique among the professions. That factor is this: we are a cross-section profession. We deal with horizontal slices of life, cut thick or thin but never present in entirety. The child comes to us out of limbo, a *terra incognita* which can be mapped and charted only fuzzily with the dubious assistance of the cumulative record folder. He leaves us after a brief but eventful span, passing like Arthur to an unknown bourn where we cannot follow, and from which seep down to us only the rarest and most tantalizing glimpses of a future we were never meant to share.

Unless we achieve a sort of quasi-immortality, like

Mr. Chips, and live to see the grandchildren of our pupils come back to us like a kind of human compound interest, we seldom achieve fulfillment. We are in the exact position of a Hitchcock fan condemned to watch the reshowing of the first reel over and over again, but who never gets to see how the mystery comes out. Once in a while a headline will open up a glimpse or two. A former student becomes an eminent politician. Another locksteps into the death chamber at San Quentin. Out of the hundreds whose lives we have so intimately affected, what are these few bones thrown us by a careless future? Some of us get letters. Some have visitors. More of us do not.

Is this frustration? Why, it is the delirious ultimate in frustration. It is the psychiatrist's happy hunting ground. Here we shall let him take over and tell us what comes next.

"That's rather obvious," he remarks, beaming at us over his spectacles and smoothing down the cushions of his couch. "Sublimation, of course. Substitution, if you like that better."

And so we substitute.

Where the family doctor receives the tearful thanks of the patient whose life he has saved, we set up various societal mechanisms so that we can thank each other. The lawyer who succeeds in removing his client from immediate proximity to the hot seat gets his sense of completion well fortified with testimonial dinners, hearty appreciation, and something considerably more substantial. An educator gets another degree. If he is lucky and hits the jackpot, other educators conspire together and award him a scholarship

to some institution of higher learning where he can ac-
cumulate still more of those scrolls and parchments which
have come to symbolize fulfillment in our profession.

Our friendly psychiatrist is still smiling at us. After all,
it is seldom that he gets to analyze an entire profession.

"You see, your frustration is fundamental—built in. The
human brain is not constructed to contemplate infinity
without showing signs of drastic wear and tear. And your
job involves infinity."

The physician cures or kills. His job ends with the discharge of his patient, into the bosom of his family or of
Abraham, as the case may be.

The attorney wins or loses. His appeals, though seemingly interminable, are finite.

The engineer dedicates his bridge. The ribbon is cut, the
traffic roars by, he goes home to dinner.

Where does our job end?

Certainly it does not end with the promotion of the
pupil. The seeds which we have sown have hardly begun to
germinate by that time. They may ripen by years, by
decades, or not at all. Like Tennyson's world, the rever-
berations of our teaching spin forever down the ringing
grooves of change. We, however, are seldom around to
catch the echoes.

It is doubtful if Aristotle with all his wisdom could have
imagined the Hellenization of the known world which
sprang from the short years he spent teaching the youthful
Alexander. Mentor Graham was shoveled into an unknown
grave, unremembered save by that single pupil whose voice,
framing the imperishable syllables "of the people, by the
people, for the people" gave back to mankind thoughts

implanted years before by the humble Illinois instructor. The ripples of that teaching have not yet ceased to widen in the pool of history. Who is to say what their final implication may prove to be?

All of us in Education are engaged in an endless game of blind-man's buff with the future. Fruition, completion, fulfillment—these concomitants of other life work are not for us. The shadowy form of the psychiatrist in the background, nodding pleasantly like a metronome, reminds us of our fate.

We must substitute, or suffer the consequences.

And for what fetishes have we been content to trade the future? Conventions and conferences, for one thing. Was ever any profession so bespangled calendar-wise with dates of workshops, institutes, meetings, and buzz sessions? From these semiannual swarmings emerge clouds of mimeographed summaries, dittoed synopses, and printed yearbooks, studded with those most heart-warming of all symbols—our names.

Then there are the degrees and credentials. These also bear our names, along with other formulas and incantations designed to impress both contemporaries and posterity. In the light of the frequently heard murmur that all it takes to get any such document under the sun are sufficient funds and the patience of Job, what is the significance of these pieces of paper? Once again, it is symbolism. They represent status, prestige, appreciation—the poor crutches which replace the nonexistent limbs of completion and fulfillment.

To resort to imperfect analogy, let us visualize an imaginary medical profession wherein no doctor ever knew whether his patients lived or died, wherein the diagnosis was neither verified nor disproved, wherein after treating the ailment the physician had to depend upon the uncertain vagaries of correspondence, rumor, and the press to discover the final outcome of the case. Nay, worse still, by some miraculous process of eugenics the treatment of the patient affected his very germ plasm, so that the ultimate results of the medicament became apparent only in the second and third generation. Would not our friends the doctors throw up their hands in despair of ever knowing beyond peradventure that their theories were in fact correct? Would they not grow increasingly myopic trying to peer beyond the veil of the future? Would they not, in short, become frustrated?

I can guess what they would do to compensate. They would proliferate their medical association into unnumbered splinter groups and societies, with alphabetical initials unknown in their profusion since the early days of the New Deal. They would meet at increasingly short intervals to give testimonials to themselves and to pin medals on each other's chests. They would set up artificial hurdles along the track of life at places cunningly selected to stimulate the flagging practitioner. They would prick and goad and spur with paper rowels the laggards of their kind. They would do all those things which man devises to make up for an essential lack. They would, in all honesty, act just like us.

For we are doing all this to compensate. And indeed some form of compensatory activity is inevitable. We have to convince ourselves that our work is fundamentally important, though we lack the essential ingredient of proof. We must, if we are to continue to live with ourselves, justify the vital import of what we are doing. The sad part of it is that, while some sort of compensatory activity is no doubt essential, the self-testimonial type is definitely not.

There are other things in Education than grades and units and degrees and credentials and summer sessions. At a recent meeting of administrators and school board members, a summary of the various philosophies of Education was succinctly given, and a show of hands was called for on the part of those present who agreed basically with one or more of the major theories. Out of 200 and more at the meeting, exactly eleven responded. The others had no philosophy at all. If they did have one, it had never been taken in hand and smoothed into shape sufficiently to make it recognizable even to an expert. Here, then, were 189 of us who might profitably have taken a couple of years off from extension courses and six-week sessions to do a little old-fashioned hard thinking. I wonder how many more of us there are in this business who have never troubled to think out our intellectual responses to the challenges of Education.

We can attend to our own cultural lacks. An awful lot of us can't spell or punctuate or write grammatical paragraphs. The cure for this condition may not be as much fun as acting as an auditor at a conference brainstorming session, but as a lastingly worthwhile compensatory activity, it wins hands down.

We can add a moral tone to our communities and neighborhoods which all too many of them sadly lack.

We can become increasingly thorough students of child psychology, so that we may help to straighten the twisted lives so many homes send us.

All these things we can do to fill the void within us. But these are the very things we do not do. We substitute buttons and bows for fruition and completion, gauds for certainties, spangles for the future.

When we face up to the reality which underlies our job, to the innate incompleteness of our work, to the basic frustration of our daily tasks, then will we become a profession indeed.

► *In all the sound and fury of the last three decades, few stopped to ponder the almost imperceptible metamorphosis of the School Administrator. From a scholarly, substantial original there evolved a brisk, highly nervous type, complete with flashing teeth, gray flannel suit, and a complete set of canned responses to any given questions. This, too, was Nobody's fault—but the transformation was typical of the times. . . .*

Open Season

9

THE COOL, CRISP days of fall are with us again. The smell of wood smoke fills the air, and the voice of the huntsman is heard in the land. The baying of the taxpayer association pack mingles distantly and musically with the cheery shouts of the school improvement committee beaters as they come excitedly upon the spoor they have been seeking. Presently the unfortunate quarry breaks cover, panting and blowing, and silhouettes himself for an unwise moment atop the nearest rise of land. The "view halloa" sounds, the crash of the discharge echoes shudderingly through the peaceful countryside, and another fine, fat school superintendent kicks convulsively for a moment, only to lie at last quite still, ready for the flaying.

Occasionally the intended victim is merely winged, or perhaps startled out of his wits by a near miss. In such an event, he may be expected to take cover at once where the greenery is thickest, usually in the lush mazes afforded by the education department of the nearest university. He may, in fact, lie doggo in such a sanctuary for years, sheltered beneath the comforting protection of the doctoral degree and nourished by occasional consultantships. The principle of protective coloration will sometimes permit him to escape destruction by passing as a principal or dean, or even an administrative assistant, for the remainder of his harried life. Inexorably, however, the casualty lists continue to grow, and the future of this highly developed species seems regrettably uncertain.

There is a certain horrid fascination inherent in any study of a dying order. Gibbon made a life work and a reputation out of Rome's collapse, and Spengler did much the same on a somewhat broader and more modern scale. Somehow it is always easier to peddle dissertations on decay than homilies on health. But it's a messy business at best, and in discussing the decline and fall of the superintendency from the standpoint of one of the decliners and fallers, I feel unpleasantly like a member of the Seventh Cavalry writing on his knapsack about Custer's Last Stand while the shooting is still in progress.

For Top Administration is undeniably in a bad way. We're becoming scarce and hard to flush, fellows, even in our natural habitat. It is not so much that in many states the number of school districts has decreased sharply in recent years as a result of consolidation, although this trend is undeniably contributing to the growing rarity of *genus superintendensis*. It is rather that evolutionary processes, aided, I fear, by our own inadequacies, seem to be culminating in such an overly specialized breed that, like the dinosaurs, we may be evolving ourselves out of existence.

Survival of the fittest has always implied a high mortality rate. Thomas Huxley used to plug Darwinism with a series of lethal sideswipes at some of that doctrine's stuffier and more costive opponents. One of his mordant quips may be relevant today.

"The cradle of every science," he would chortle to a discomfited audience of reverend graybeards, "is surrounded by dead theologians as that of Hercules was with strangled serpents."

It is perhaps more than mere coincidence that America's first school superintendent was appointed the same year that Darwin returned from his famous voyage in the *Beagle*. The profession of school administration, like the theory of natural selection, is thus relatively new. Unfortunately, the corpses surrounding its bassinet are neither departed clergymen nor garrotted snakes. To put it ungrammatically but bluntly, they are us.

The *Beagle's* noted passenger found that a species might be erased over a given period of time by either of two processes: a wrong turn in evolutionary development, or the continuing attacks of an enemy against whom it has no adequate defense. It seems to me that Top Administration in this country has accelerated unwarrantedly the race toward extinction by becoming a sitting duck for both processes at once.

And—as a prospective fossil—I protest.

In doing so, I am aware that an articulate woolly mammoth or a philosophical passenger pigeon undoubtedly would have voiced a similar complaint, and with at least equal justice. Nevertheless I am reluctant to believe that so lordly and majestic a creature as the superintendent of schools is destined to perish wholly from his present haunts, leaving but a few ossified remains for future scholars to ponder over. Surely, I keep telling myself, in the inscrutable design of Providence there must somewhere be a place— no matter how remote and inaccessible—where these fast-thinning herds can find refuge, not only from the implacable foes whose sport they have become but also from the wrenching stresses of an environment to which they are becoming increasingly unadapted.

It will, however, take more than wishful thinking—more even than our present restless and never-ending migrations from position to position over the face of the earth—to preserve our kind from the fate which overtook the great auk. In the manner of evolution's distinguished discoverer, then, let us try to survey the factors underlying our present predicament in the hope that we may be able in some way to forestall the ominous beckoning of the future.

First off, the nature of the job has changed. A generation or two ago, Top Administration rose loftily above the gently rolling educational foothills, its slopes teeming with a luxuriant growth of aspiring vice-principals and supervisors and its peak mantled with the eternal whiteness of universal respect. At irregular intervals, the mountain would shake and rumble, a ruddy glow would couple with a smoky column to draw attention to the summit, and the latest addenda to school policy would be handed down by relays of Moseses and Joshuas to the hushed and reverent folk clustered at the bottom. There was as little prospect for any drastic change in higher personnel as there was that some wandering Mohammed would successfully command the whole vast formation to hie itself beyond the horizon.

The topography has changed dramatically of late. The coming of the Democratic Education glacier has eroded the once mighty peak down to the level of the gentle hills which once it dominated. The eye of the traveler, vainly seeking a cynosure whereon it might rest in grateful contemplation, finds instead merely another mound nestling snugly among its peers. It may be a very useful little hillock, but it is hardly apt to inspire the awe which clung about its predecessor. Indeed, it is distressingly subject to subdividing, bulldozing, or even plowing under to make room for the structural whims of its inhabitants. It is especially vulnerable to organized attack, since it retains to a large extent the aura of responsibility which attached to it in the days of its majesty. Any little earth tremor is apt to bring out the power graders and the steam shovels in full cry.

"The king reigns, but he does not rule."

He is still subject to regicide, however. . . .

The on-going, forward-looking, in-grouping school district of today is administered not by a superintendent but by a series of staff committees. They screen new hires, set up in-service training programs, establish discipline standards, recommend salaries, conduct building surveys, and inspect the plumbing. All of them are democratic, some of them are industrious, and a few of them are competent. The one thing which all of them have in common is a nimble agility in scuttling speedily out from under the blame which inevitably follows their far-from-occasional bloopers. Public chastisement then seeks out its traditional target, and the well-meaning administrator who has been standing by benevolently and *ex officio* while one busy faculty group collects the sulphur, another accumulates the saltpeter, and still a third adds the charcoal finds himself all alone holding the cannon cracker when it goes off in his face.

It is, after all, almost impossible to fire a committee.

Then there is the little matter of tenure. It can be summarized easily by saying that the teacher has it and the administrator hasn't. In a growing number of states, tenure laws are helping to kill off the superintendent by making it impossible to excise or seriously to influence the very people for whom the citizenry holds him responsible. In all the brouhaha over tenure during the past few years, the impossible position in which it has placed the administrator has been consistently underplayed. Certain situations arise from time to time in our line of business which practically demand that someone get the ax.

Old Miss Smith may start falling asleep in the middle of the reading circle.

Young Mr. Jones may spend more and more time reading Mickey Spillane to his trigonometry class.

Parents seethe. The Board erupts. Someone's hide is clearly called for. In states where Smitty and Jonesy can thumb their noses at the world behind the Maginot Line of tenure, you can guess who eventually gets the sack.

Despite the manifold blessings conferred by the recent egalitarian trend in our profession, then, there are still one or two problems stridently clamoring for solution if Democratic Education is not to come a cropper. Top Administration, to switch metaphors completely, has come of late to resemble the coy stripteaser on the burlesque runway who endears herself progressively to the baldheaded row with each garment of authority which she discards, only to be yanked off by the gendarmes to the local bastille when she finally arrives at the ultimate in undress.

In short, we are damned if we don't and fired if we do.

But our underlying problem is far graver than that posed

by the steadily falling temperatures of an unfriendly professional climate. The truth is that, like the protagonists of classic Greek drama, we carry within ourselves the seeds of our own dissolution.

One of these tragic flaws is the means we have adopted for perpetuating our profession. Without the slightest evidence to support the myth that an above-average teacher will necessarily or even probably be a good administrator, we have been raiding our classrooms of their most talented instructors for years in order to augment our ranks. How often we have been left holding the bag, wondering why an ex-teacher (who took up the career in the first place because he was introverted, studious, and retiring) turned out to be such a lousy administrator.

In an effort to wriggle off this horn of the dilemma, we have too often turned to more overt and kinetic types, such as ex-football coaches and athletic directors, trusting to meaty muscles to erect an impressive curriculum and to stentorian voices to call forth effective public relations. Here too we have had occasion more than once to ponder the unaccountable failure of a mighty molder of varsity teams when confronted with such relatively common administrative problems as employee rating, regional accreditation, and political pressure groups.

Survival of the fittest? Rather its antithesis.

Even if it is true—which I do not for one moment believe —that success in administration depends upon ability to compromise, to slither dexterously among the points of the educational compass, to be all things to all people, then we are certainly selecting strange successors to follow us. Those of us charged with the duty of culling and training the future leaders of the profession have failed even to take the first and most necessary step. We have not decided whether we want to breed lions or eels. Small wonder that the products of such a slap-dash system frequently resemble something out of Ovid's *Metamorphoses*.

Our trouble is that no one has been willing to sit down and think out logically a pattern for Top Administration. We need to know what the superintendent should *do* before we can say with any degree of confidence what he should *be*.

One concept makes him the Man with the Oil Can. The school system is envisioned as a complex machine with many moving parts, one cog grinding against another, engendering inescapable friction. Increased heat results when what is wanted is increased power. Unless the friction can be removed or minimized, a breakdown will sooner or later occur. Here is where the Man with the Oil Can comes into the picture, moving ceaselessly up and down the long assembly line of clicking, whirring parts, searching endlessly for signs of wear, applying to the best of his judgment the soothing lubricants of praise, tolerance, justice, and human kindness.

Such a concept of the superintendency is not an ignoble one. It is even accurate as far as it goes. Its limitation lies in its equation of our profession with a machine and Top Administration with skilled labor.

Administration is—or should be—infinitely more than a collection of skills. Our techniques are ministered to by the combined education faculties of a hundred universities. We can measure standard deviations in a flash. We can speak with confidence of assessed valuations, site drainage, and dry-wall construction. We are more competent in a score of areas than the men who came before us. Yet our hold upon the people becomes ever less certain, our existence more precarious.

I offer you at once an hypothesis and a paradox: though we need to know what we *do* before we can know what we *are*, we are battling extinction not because of what we *do* but because of what we *are*.

Our forebears in this business were, whether we like the idea or not, men of pith and substance. They were so regarded by the public which retained them in office for decades on end. So secure were they in their positions and prestige that they found ample leisure to cultivate impressive beards and, in later life, imposing bay windows. They exuded an aura of permanence and solidity. Contrast these patriarchs with their slick modern counterparts in administrative positions, so many of them fast-moving, fast-talking, fast-changing.

What has brought about the transformation? Is it not—more than anything else—the hard-to-face truth that the trail blazers in our profession were learned men, and that we, whatever else we may be, are certainly not that?

Consider this:

They knew little of topological and vector psychology—but they could write perfect English.

They were naive in their ideas of public relations—but they could read the Iliad *in Greek and the* Aeneid *in Latin.*

They were mere babes when it came to equalization formulas—but they were fluent in art, in music, in history, in philosophy.

Here, I believe, is the nub of the whole matter. People

admired and respected and looked up to our predecessors as the cultural leaders of their communities. They represented Education magnificently because they *were* educated.

What are we respected for? Our knowledge of acoustic tiles? Our ability to draw up transportation routes? Our facility with lunchroom counts?

Instead of adding the competencies of the present to the wisdom of the past, we have been content to substitute. And therein lies our heel of Achilles, our rift in the lute, our leak in the dyke. When we permitted ourselves this fatal luxury we diverged from the fruitful and productive path of evolution, and entered upon the sterile season of our present discontent. Unless we can somehow find the upward trail we left a generation ago, we are doomed to wander endlessly from pillar to post, from job to dwindling job.

Legend has it that when the Pied Piper lured the children of Hamelin into the bowels of Koppelberg Hill, he led them by dark and devious underground ways into a new and enchanted land, bright with the colors of the rainbow and echoing with the song of birds. We schoolmen find ourselves in like case, shepherding our clamorous school districts through a succession of dank corridors, murky and shadowy, lined with the bits of rubbish for which we have bartered away our birthright. Here and there among the quaint debris which once seemed so important to us we pass a shattered toy stamped "Group Dynamics." Here again we come upon a broken teeter-totter tagged "Meeting Felt Needs." A little farther along sprawls a moth-eaten raccoon coat, relic of the 1920s, and on it the soiled and ragged label, "Bridging the Gap."

As we pass with our demanding and noisy charges among the scattered and woebegone clichés, relics of a bygone era, there appears far down the darkened passageway a narrow chink of light, widening from moment to moment and flooding the gloom with blinding radiance. The great bronze doors which mark the gateway to the future are slowly swinging on their iron hinges. Through the slender portal thus created come strange sights and bewildering sounds—the rumble of awesome machines, the dazzle and sparkle of undreamed-of structures, the crimson glare of rockets, the silver trail of satellites. With every step the doorway widens and the flood of light intensifies.

Educators, friends of education, administrators of education all over the land:

We know that all too soon we must go beyond that door. We know, too, that the future will simultaneously require our profession to enter upon its next stage of evolutionary development in order to meet the unguessable challenge of tomorrow. We have every reason to believe that it will take all the massed wisdom of our cultural heritage to surmount that challenge.

How are we fixed for survival?

While struggling with its own self-engendered problems, Education had also to cope with the calculated attacks of the Ax-Grinders. Millions of people were honestly concerned with what was happening in the schools. But there were a good many, too, who saw in the growing crisis a golden opportunity to do Education in. Thus the profession found itself in the position of the elephant which has blundered through its own ineptness into a quagmire, and now finds itself beset by opportunistic Pygmies equipped with poison arrows. . . .

10

> *In the beginning were Chaos and old*
> *Night, brooding over the formless embryos*
> *of Time and Space. From the abyss of Void*
> *and Mass and Darkness issued in good time*
> *the two great Principles of the Universe—*
> *Female, in the fertile form of Gaea, Earth;*
> *Male, vaulting immensely over his spacious*
> *partner in the shape of Uranus, Heaven.*
> *The union brought forth gods and monsters,*
> *men and beasts. Most savage and cunning*
> *among the offspring of Uranus were the*
> *Titans, instigators of hate and strife. Varied*
> *were they in form, and clamorous in many*
> *tongues, but united in a sullen hatred of*
> *their great father. Under the leadership of*
> *Cronus the crafty, they lay in wait for their*
> *sire with an iron sickle, and drove him*
> *forever from the affairs of Creation, bleed-*
> *ing and eternally emasculate.*
>
> —HESIOD

HAVE YOU TAKEN time out recently to contemplate the enemies of Education? I don't mean to duck; all of us do that often enough, and almost automatically. I mean to analyze the Opposition.

They're quite a crew. Like the legendary Titans, they take many shapes and speak with changing voices. But they were all our children, once. In their day, they swung like amiable gibbons from our jungle gyms, raced through dusty halls in glad defiance of the rules, and shuffled their feet in immemorial fashion beneath our classroom desks.

What they learned, they learned from us. The specious arguments they raise in the committee rooms of Congress ring with our accent. Their glib pronouncements in the popular periodicals are peppered with our punctuation, garnished with our grammar, and salted with the style we taught them not so long ago. We look on them now with a sort of numb dismay, recognizing in their distorted faces and crooked gestures a macabre mixture of our own features and those of the children who once they were, even as reflections in fun-house mirrors give back lethal caricatures of the observer plus a sinister something more.

Examine with me, if you will, these children of ours, grown now to man's estate, and sharpening their sickles.

THE HYPOCRITES

These are the most charming of the Enemy. They wear Brooks Bros. suits. They patronize the best barbers. They are hired expensively and owned completely by the several manufacturers' associations and national chambers. They are dedicated to the proposition that nothing is too good for Education except money.

The Hypocrites learned much from us. They turn out slick booklets tastefully designed to show the ardent support of their companies for the schools. They are experts at constructing tables and charts illustrating in living color how (1) Education is good for Business, (2) Business is good to Education, and (3) therefore everything is going to be just dandy.

The smiles become a little strained and the back-slapping falls off sharply when a move is made to channel a little more of the national wealth into the schools, however. Need you guess whom we see then before the congressional committees, damning with faint praise and stifling with sneers of slow disparagement? Their techniques are impeccable, and damnably effective—the two-martini luncheon, the reminiscences about the good old days before life became complex and the schools expensive.

Then there are the slogans. Like Jimmy Durante, they've got a million of 'em.

"Kids don't need to go to school in palaces."

"Teaching is only a part-time job."

"Keep local taxes low."

It works. These gray-flanneled Ivy League types with their Madison Avenue methods have helped keep the United States a nation which spends more on its sinning than it does on its schooling, far more on its luxuries than on its learning. They can sell anything but the truth. This is unsellable, because it is simply that more money spent on education might keep their well-heeled employers from buying that new yacht or taking that annual trip to the Riviera.

Let us leave these false friends, who come before the nation bearing flattering brochures in one hand and the old stiletto in the other.

Dante placed the hypocrites in Gulf Six, Circle Eight of his Inferno. There they were burdened with intolerable weights. I suppose that we may as well derive what comfort we can from the thought that in some future hell of their own making these smooth, soft-tongued, slippery saboteurs are going to be really loaded.

THE INGRATES

Not too many years ago, a doctoral study was made in Los Angeles which examined the educational pattern of voting precincts. Special attention was given to the way the voters in these districts reacted to school finance measures. Each precinct was identified in accordance with its educational level. If most of its voters were college graduates, it was a "high" precinct. Those made up largely of people with high-school backgrounds were labeled "middle," and those benighted areas whose inhabitants had just made it through grade school were, naturally enough, "low."

The results were fascinating.

The "high" precincts turned out *en masse* on election day and used their college-trained minds to vote solidly against school bonds and tax increases in any form for any reason.

The "middle" voters divided half and half on issues involving more money for the schools. It would be consoling, but probably misleading, to attribute this division to the "suspension of judgment" recommended by certain of the great philosophers.

So it was left to the electors of the "low" precincts to swing the balance for the kids, and they did exactly that. The ignorant, the quasi-illiterate, the cultural Philistine—

these least educated of Americans supported their schools most faithfully.

Here is irony worthy of Dean Swift. Those who had profited most from Education, who had lived in Education's house and supped at Education's table, who of all men had most reason to respect and uphold and cherish Education were the first to welsh on their benefactor when the time came to stand up and be counted. Those who had learned the least and benefited the least from Education rallied to its side and upheld a cause otherwise lost indeed.

Extrapolation is perilous here. It leads to the inevitable conclusion that the more people we educate, the less support we can expect to have. The better we teach, the more the schools will be allowed to deteriorate. The higher the educational level we are able to bring about, the lower will be the national opinion of public instruction. This way madness lies. We had better give it up, and quote Mark Twain:

"If you pick up a starving dog and make him prosperous, he will not bite you. This is the principal difference between a dog and a man."

It's either grin or succumb to tears of self-pity while ingratitude, more strong than traitors' arms, quite vanquishes us.

THE QUITTERS

When part of an army lights out for the rear in the midst of a battle, it is a tired truism that a greater burden is

thrown on the remaining troops. The load is doubly oner-
ous when the deserters have been highly trained specialists.

It distresses me to have you take some of America's
churches as an example. For some time now they have been
bawling for school money, whining for released time, and
pouting because Bible commentaries are not being read daily
to school children. This somewhat infantile display of
temper has served to conceal but not to efface the fact that
many of our reverend colleagues have fallen down on the
job. A generation or two ago they had no need to clamor
for such artificial respiration. They were doing a job, and
their churches were full. Today they seek a captive congre-
gation and a privileged place at the public trough. These
things they may get, but at the cost of their heritage. They
will have abdicated their position in the front ranks for a
cushy spot in the rear echelon.

There are all kinds of people who want to stop working
and let the schools take over for them. Public safety bureau-
crats in fifty states don't want to teach their citizens to
navigate their highways successfully, so they arrange for
the school people to include driver training in an already
bogged-down curriculum. Podunk wants organized recreation, but doesn't want the headaches of handling it. So
Education wryly welcomes another freeloader. Uncle Sam
hesitates to ask too much directly of our Spartan youth, so
the high schools get cadet corps and ROTC.

All this wouldn't be so bad if we got any thanks for it.
But you know what we get.

"Too many frills. Too much money spent on non-
essentials. Not enough time spent on fundamentals. The
school has its nose in everything."

Of course there is a solution. Let the Quitters take back their babies and nurse them themselves.

You say this will never happen? Oh, well. I didn't say it was a *practical* solution.

THE PINHEADS

Sooner or later, every schoolman runs up against the fiery-eyed, gibberish-muttering, rattlesnake-handling brothers and sisters of the Lunatic Fringe. These zealous zanies are visited upon the profession for no apparent reason at all, as boils were bestowed upon Job.

The Pinheads have a devastating approach. They appeal not to your intellect but to your conscience. This at once places someone like me at a considerable disadvantage, because I have never been entirely certain that I possessed this delicate commodity. And they follow through relentlessly.

Are you building a new gym? You will be buttonholed by a committee of lank-haired elders. They will want a separate, enclosed, coffinlike shower-and-dressing room for each girl, despite the architectural and financial enormity of the mere idea. If you resist the demand, then you are a son of Belial, lustfully relishing the unspeakable thoughts arising in the minds of fifteen-year-old girls at the sight of each other's naked bodies.

Is your girls' physical education instructor teaching her kids the Virginia reel? She'd better not be if there are any Pinheads in town. Everyone knows that dancing is a device of Satan. To hear the Pinheads talk, the damned souls in Hell must spend every nonfrying moment tangoing or turkey trotting. When you stop to think about it, this conjures up a delightfully bizarre picture of the Nether Regions which almost reconciles me to the probability of someday visiting them.

Are you saluting the flag, singing Christmas carols, or studying evolution? Some nut is almost sure to blow the whistle on you.

Did you ever pause to wonder what all these cockeyed crusaders have against the schools? The answer is simple. They hate and fear them, because Education will eventully destroy them and the creepy causes they uphold. Science and logic and knowledge are anathema to the Pinhead, and for obvious reasons. He stands for bigotry and superstition. Education blocks his path to the minds and hearts of the children.

He hates the schools the way a fly hates the swatter.

There are other enemies of Education, of course. There are the Ax-Grinders and the Profiteers and the Mossbacks. There are the Demagogues and the Ward-Heelers. Their eyes bulge out at us from the fun-house mirrors. The congested veins cord like Medusa's snakes from the foreheads wavering in the curving glass. We turn away and go out into the cool of the evening, appalled at the contortions of the massed reflections.

"How," my colleagues and I ask ourselves pathetically, "has a profession which strives only to do good and tell the truth accumulated such enemies?"

Well, now—let's not get sickening about it, as someone

else has said. A lot of this is our own fault. We have striven too long and too hard to be all things to all people. We have been guilty, too, of the sin of Pride. We have been willing to see Education gorged with all sorts of extraneous projects and problems until it swelled like a force-fed goose. Conversely, we have been unwilling or unable to state our case to the American people strikingly enough to silence our foes.

But our greatest mistake has been the image of Education which we have presented to the nation. It has been for a generation and more an essentially feminine image—gentle, noncombative, benevolent, maternal, a little fussy.

With all due respect to the thousands of devoted and dedicated women who labor so diligently in our countless classrooms, Education is not feminine. Since the days of Socrates and Plato and before, it has been masculine in its outlook and appeal. Until just yesterday, it has always been so in our own country. It seeks to change concepts, to conquer ignorance, to fight evil. It brings not peace but a sword. In its final, triumphant form, it will sweep the planet like some mighty besom, smashing the dykes and levees of folly like matchwood and fulfiling its ancient role as the guardian and mentor of the human race.

Yes, Education is male.

But so was Father Uranus.

We had better keep an eye on our children. Especially the ones with the sickles. . . .

► *In fact, there are times when it is difficult to determine whether or not Education is more sinned against than sinning. Certainly the post-Sputnik discovery by the American people that their educational system left something to be desired was more reflex than reflection. But the hysterical attacks upon the profession, root and branch, did perhaps more harm than good. And the uncritical willingness to attribute almost magical qualities to the educational methods of our great Enemy was clearly out of line.*

The Scapegoat

11

WE AMERICANS ARE a lighthearted lot.

It has been over fifteen years now since the first hammerings and poundings began to pulse out of the dark and somewhat noisome Soviet cave across the gully, and the faint traceries of smoke against the Eurasian sky heralded the coming of technology to what had always been essentially a Neanderthal state. The rumble of the embryonic assembly lines and the tentative peepings of a fledgling science aroused a certain mild, almost tolerant interest among some of our industrialists and statesmen reminiscent of nothing so much as the amused scoffing with which these same gentlemen had saluted the rise of Hitler's Germany. The offstage sound effects of rifle volleys and whistling knouts which punctuated the promising rumblings and peepings did little to encourage our closer interest and much to strengthen our skepticism.

After all, there was nothing to alarm the richest, strongest, best-advertised country in the world, was there? Everybody knew the Russians were backward. Their automobiles were ten years behind ours, especially in the all-important field of tail fins. Their television sets were few and far between, and entirely lacked the essential feature of color. They seemed virtually incapable of training such high-priority citizens as movie stars and baseball players. Worst of all and significant of the direst national retardation was the almost total absence of many of life's minimum essentials—things like lipstick, falsies, and Coca-Cola.

But if the Russians dropped an iron curtain around themselves in the mid-1940s, behind which they built and starved and plotted, we erected around our satisfied selves a picket fence composed of chrome bumpers, king-size filter tips, and empty bottles of imported Scotch whisky behind which we—quite frankly—had fun. We had, it is true, a few serious moments. In our spare time we gave away a good many billions of dollars to questionable foreigners for purposes which were somewhat obscure to the average taxpayer, and we blithely permitted an almost unlimited number of mangy Commy agents free access to what we laughingly called our atomic secrets.

But nothing was taken too seriously. Nothing was allowed to disturb our composure. Above all, no hint of coming austerity or sacrifice was suffered to ripple even for a moment the brimming pool of full prosperity.

In short, we were strutting, free-wheeling specimens on a grand scale of what the old Greeks used to call *hubris*, that fatal pride in one's own excellence which in classical times used to call for immediate chastisement with one of Jove's more lethal thunderbolts. To mix metaphors, our necks were out and we were riding for a fall.

Into this smug smog of perfumed complacency has driven like a stiff breeze from the north the recent and startling achievements of Soviet science. In glistening silver letters traced across the sky for all to see, the Russian satellites and moon rockets have written *Finis* to our dream of a monopoly of know-how. The time is obviously here for a girding of loins and a measured marshaling of our resources in preparation for a technological marathon which may last a hundred years. Clear thinking and a calm evaluation of an extremely tricky long-range problem are now imperative for our survival as a nation.

So, instead of thoughtful determination, what symptoms have marked our reaction to the totalitarian threat? The old Shakespearian phrase "alarums and excursions" best describes it.

Our Democratic politicians have accused their Republican counterparts of sabotaging national defense in the name of economy. The Republicans point reproving fingers at long years of Democratic neglect. Both have seized frantically upon our traditional American panacea for all the ills that flesh is heir to: unlimited spending.

Big business is charged with monopolistic practices and an unduly greedy attention to profits.

Labor stands before a dozen investigating committees, heckled with accusations of corruption and condemned for rising prices.

The Army fights guerrilla battles against the Air Force more acrimoniously than it ever did against the Indians, and both services combine furiously against the threat posed by the Navy's Vanguard missile and atomic subs to their internecine struggle for the lion's share of the tax dollar. It is a perfectly ridiculous spectacle and, under other circumstances of less urgency, would be good for a whole volley of therapeutic belly laughs.

There is one culprit, however, against whom all the warring factions of our society have been able to unite. A crisis demands a scapegoat, and in this case the hapless animal is already staked out and waiting for the ax. In choosing a burnt offering, of course, it always helps to select an individual or a group which has been importunate or embarrassing to the majority of the citizenry. It is even better when the potential target is essentially pacifistic and defenseless. And it is pure icing on the cake when the victim-to-be has had the temerity to be expensive and the bad judgment to call attention to its needs.

The scapegoat charged with responsibility for our current posture of scientific inadequacy is, needless to say, the American public school system. It is a natural for the role of patsy. Within the past few years, it has been blamed successively for juvenile delinquency, the shortage of engineers, the rise of comic books, high taxes, and Elvis Presley. Surely, reasoned the harried searchers for an easy out, the schools could shoulder one more load.

To put it bluntly, educators were elected by acclamation to be the fall guys for the nation's criminal negligence. We are supposed to be the pigeons.

Well, I for one am not having any. There are lots of stupid, chuckleheaded things that my profession has been guilty of during the past three decades, and I have spent a good deal of time chastising with the valor of my tongue what I have considered to be its errors. I have been audibly impatient with the snail creep of its progress and the limitless inertia of its thought. With several others, I have complained and crusaded and needled. I have been part of the loyal opposition.

But this attack is different.

It is selfish and cold-blooded. It is intentionally and deliberately unfair.

It uses loaded statistics to shoot down straw men. It claims, for example, that a smaller percentage of children are studying science than in the past, but carefully overlooks the fact that the unprecedented inundation of the schools by millions of unlooked-for pupils has rendered all such percentage losses as inevitable as they are inconsequential.

It blasts the profession for failure to provide inspirational teaching, purposely forgetting that massed raids upon our ranks by businessmen and industrialists waving thousand-dollar bills have extracted from our classrooms as though with forceps much of our finest instructional material.

It sneers at the faltering achievement level of some of our high-school pupils, neglecting to mention that for the first time in the million-year history of the human race a nation has laid upon its teachers the crushing task of educating not only the wealthy, the congenial, and the gifted, but also the morons, the criminals, the depraved, and—worst of all—the uninterested.

Is it the fault of Education that Americans have been more interested in making a fast buck than in sending a manned rocket to the moon?

Can educators be blamed because this country has, since pioneer days, periodically exhibited a strongly anti-intellectual bias which has glorified the sharp operator and belittled the scholar?

Do we have to stand still for the charge that our profesional leaders have engaged in a premeditated conspiracy to water down the instructional program to the point where we will be a pushover for the Russians?

I say that we do not.

For a little over a generation now, the nation's schools have been locked in a titanic struggle with the problems spawned by universal education. During this time, mistakes have been made, but they have been mistakes always of the head, never of the heart. We have erred almost always on the side of optimism, seldom on the side of pessimism.

We have taught our children to be self-reliant. If the American soldier is the most ingenious and imaginative fighter in the history of warfare, as many military experts aver, he developed these qualities in American schools. When the chips are down, as God grant they may never be, and when the robot masses of Eurasia confront for the first time the inventiveness and competence of the American fighting man, we may be sure that the lessons learned in the very educational institutions now under such vindictive attack will see the nation through.

We have taught our children to think democratically. Through wars and rumors of wars, inflation and depression, fair weather and foul, we have successfully resisted the temptation to retrace the easy, bad old road to authoritarianism. It has not been the American people who have coldly bent subject nations to their whim, nor have we contemptuously used our power to grind out a despairing obedience from those who hate us. It took another educational philosophy than ours to produce behind the Iron Curtain this soulless cynicism.

We have taught our children to be decent, kindly, and charitable. There has never been an appeal made to us, from Helsinki to Chungking and all the suffering places in between, which our people have not leaped to meet. Whether it be famine or pestilence, flood or fire, it is to America that the cry is raised, and to no other. Always the need is met, the ships are loaded and sent forth, the mercy planes dispatched. When the recording angel sets down upon the brazen roll of Heaven the follies and fatuities which we have taught our pupils, surely selfishness will not be one of them.

We have taught our children to love liberty. The welfare of the individual has been our deep concern. The educators of our country, despite their faults, have never been guilty of that supreme sin against the very spirit of Education—the turning out of gray, impersonal masses of young people from our schools, dedicated only to the limitless expansion of a God-denying state. Each child is to us precious, unique. We dare not, for our souls' sake, mold him willy-nilly into a technician or a nuclear physicist or a commissar merely because the state has signified a temporary shortage. When we so prostitute our ancient calling, may a wise Providence abolish us as a profession and relegate us to the limbo of all those who have been tried and found wanting.

Our educational way of life, together with all that we work and live for, is now face to face with a supreme challenge posed by another and an alien system of instruction. In the Armageddon which seems about to engulf the planet, it will not be troops and missiles and wealth alone which will be thrown into the final scales. Education, too, will have to stand or fall on the basis of what it has added to our country's brain and nerve and sinew.

Should this, then, be a cause for doubting or self-questioning?

I fail to see why. While our judgment, being human, has erred from time to time, our intentions at least have been on the side of the angels. Our goals have been clean and honest.

And when all the cards have been placed on the table, I do not believe that we need worry overmuch about the results, despite the carpings of our frightened critics.

In the unpredictable days which lie ahead, certain things are sure. It will not be the boys now occupying the desks of our numberless classrooms who will slaughter from the safety of great tanks the freedom-seeking citizens of a persecuted land. We leave this to our "educated" enemies.

Nor will the girls now developing minds and bodies in our countless school gymnasiums be fit only to drudge their painful lives away sweeping dirty streets and straining under heavy loads. This enlightened practice we will also gladly leave to "educated" Russia.

It is highly questionable, too, whether the clear-eyed young men and women who have studied in our biology laboratories will accept in later life, Lysenko-like, the arbitrary dictum of a paranoiac politician that acquired characteristics are inherited. We will cheerfully forgo this ludicrous aspect of Soviet "education," also.

Finally, we will be able to live with ourselves, clean of the filthy knowledge that everything we have taught the boys and girls entrusted to our care has been a poisonous lie. We will not have told them that black is white, that good is evil, and that peace is war. This, too, we leave to Communist "education."

Instead, let us take comfort in the knowledge that we follow in great footsteps, that yet again the opportunity has been given to our profession to assist, with God's grace, in the saving of our country.

From beneath our countless classroom desks have passed in time gone by the feet that plodded through the mud of the Argonne and waded ashore in the bloody hell of Iwo Jima.

From the gymnasiums of American schools have come the lithe young bodies that fought and won at San Juan Hill and Tarawa, Seoul and Belleau Wood.

From the paper and pencils of our crowded classes have germinated words and thoughts destined to burgeon in time of need into great instruments for saving and for inspiration, Atlantic Charters and Four Freedoms.

From the test tubes and retorts of innumerable school laboratories have sprung the questionings and the imaginings which have culminated in the electric light, the telegraph, the protean triumphs of plastics and the ultimate marvel of thermonuclear energy.

This, then, is no time for fear of a future which with a little pluck and planning may yet be shaken from its iron groove and cast into an orbit closer to our heart's desire. It is instead a time for educators, of all men, to stand to their guns. It is a time for us to tell America not only what we have done for her but what we are prepared yet to do.

Some there is of which we need to be ashamed, and much of which we should be proud. In the past, it has been the pupils taught by our predecessors who built out of a primeval wilderness this nation which is at once the wonder and the envy of mankind. In the future, it will be the boys and girls now listening to our words who will use old earth itself as but a footstool, and who will unfurl upon the outer worlds of space the banner of the Great Republic.

► *Yet it cannot be denied that in the absence of an acceptable alternative the old, tired dogmas of Progressivism still reign in American educational strongholds. They may be camouflaged as a sort of one-world, brotherhood-of-man approach to the problems of the times. They may remain in the saddle simply because no rival philosophy has appeared to challenge them. The fact remains that the average educator in the United States is still being fed the exploded, worn-out theories of life adjustment and socialization. What is needed, of course, is a new philosophy of Education—one that will face up to the brutal truth that we are in a race with a savage foe not only for our very lives but also for our immortal souls. . . .*

UNTIL FAIRLY RECENTLY, I was superintendent of schools in a small desert community wherein dwelt a local character who rejoiced in the name of Herman. Now, Herman toiled not; neither did he spin. He did act as a sort of unofficial night watchman for some of the local businessmen, carrying at his belt an awesome array of night watchman's equipment, including a huge policeman's billy club, a two-foot flashlight, and an enormous bunch of clanking keys. In return for his nocturnal services, Herman was allowed to sleep in the rear of one of the shops, was given free run of the day-old groceries in a local market, and even was furnished with clothes by some of the kindhearted citizens who boasted a sense of humor as well as compassion.

Unfortunately, Herman was a trifle eccentric, to put it mildly. Harmless, but eccentric. In one sense, however, Herman had it all over the rest of us. It seems that years before, some officious busybody had deduced unilaterally that Herman had more than the allowable number of bats in his belfry, and had hauled him off to the booby hatch. There, to everyone's surprise, the doctors had announced firmly that Herman was legally sane, and moreover had given him a wallet-size certificate attesting to his mental

competence. This Herman carried around with him for-
evermore as his most cherished possession.

Ever afterward, whenever he became involved in a
friendly altercation and his unwary opponent disgustedly
exclaimed, "Aw, Herman, you're crazy!" Herman would
triumphantly extract the precious document from its hid-
ing place, wave it triumphantly under the nose of his
dismayed heckler, and state mildly, "I can prove *I'm* not
crazy. Where's *your* proof?"

It is this very question which I am sometimes tempted
to put to the Education profession in these United States.

Let me hasten to state that I am a member in indifferently
good standing in that profession, that almost all my friends
are similarly identified with it, and that—individually—
school people are as nice and normal a bunch of good
Americans as one could hope to find anywhere. There are
probably no more goofy educators than there are screwball
doctors or nutty lawyers—maybe not as many. Nevertheless, I am convinced that the Education profession has for
almost thirty years been behaving in a downright peculiar
fashion. And during the past fifteen, when any American
not blind drunk or moronic could have told at a glance
just by looking at the newspaper headlines once in a while
that we were heading for a life-and-death showdown with
Soviet Russia, the attitude of the so-called leaders of American Education should in my opinion have called forth the
same question that Herman used to ask his hecklers.

Sanity is a consensus. Its norms are those of the vast
majority of people at any given time. Since this is so, it
follows that the further we educators depart from the
accepted norms of society, the greater our divergence from

sanity. In areas where we have allowed ourselves to get so out of step that we are no longer even on the same street with the rest of the marchers, we are exhibiting symptoms distressingly familiar to the alert alienist.

When we attempted to minimize competition while living in a nation whose greatness was based on competition and in a world whose nations continue to compete, we were behaving irresponsibly. When we promulgated the idea that basket weaving and physics were equal in importance to the average pupil, we were being worse than irresponsible. When we told everyone that the attitudes and by-products which arose from the study of subjects were more important than the subjects themselves, we were commencing to crack badly. And when we downgraded drill, blackguarded homework, and creampuffed discipline, we were as nutty as the proverbial fruitcake.

For, by doing all these things, we widened the gap increasingly between ourselves and the citizens who supported and paid us. We have not led the parade. We have lost it somewhere back down the years. The American people, by and large, believe in competition, in the importance of subject matter per se, in discipline in the schools. It is we educators who have been saying no to all these things.

I submit that our national school curriculum, particularly in the elementary and junior high schools, has had little or no relation to the only really basic issue of the past decade and a half—national survival. Even our high schools, until the coming of Conant and the launching of Rickover's Vanguard missiles at the whole instructional program, were tripping gaily down the primrose path, encouraging pupils to take things like orientation and ceramics and stagecraft while enrollments in analytical geometry dropped off to half a dozen students per class.

The elementary course of study was where the damage was done, however. After all, the high-school academic courses, though badly shaken, did manage to survive. True, except in a relatively few institutions, two or three years of a foreign language were all you could get, and a four-year advanced mathematics program was almost unheard of. Subjects which were considered tough, like ancient history, calculus, and Latin, tended to disappear before the onslaughts of upholstering, table decorating, and second-year golf. But at least the skeleton of the time-tested secondary curriculum remained relatively intact, although it was hard to tell in many schools just where the heel bone connected to the foot bone.

But what are we to say of an official philosophy of elementary Education so ashamed of associating with history and geography that it felt compelled to drape their nudity in a grotesque Mother Hubbard called "social studies" or—worse yet—"social living"? Which found the hitherto respectable word "English" so distasteful that it substituted "language arts"? Which was horror-struck at the idea of memorizing the times tables because this would destroy the spontaneous interest of the pupil in the joyous process of multiplication?

Ironically, too, we are the very ones who have been beating the drums so loudly for "democracy in education." Had we really behaved democratically, had we gone only so far and so fast as we were able to take the American people with us, we would not now be naked to the fickle blasts of irresponsible criticism.

Let's pause just once again to stress something. The vast majority of the dedicated, hard-working teachers and principals out on the firing line were never consciously guilty of this watering-down, pablumizing process which did so much to produce a generation of quasi-illiterates. What they did, they did—most of them—on orders from above, and many of them risked their very jobs—and sometimes lost them—to smuggle nuggets of precious fact to their bewildered pupils. The tragic responsibility for this emasculation of the schools should be placed squarely where it belongs, upon the shoulders of our so-called educational leaders—men like Kilpatrick and Counts and Rugg—who swallowed hook, line, and sinker the philosophy of John Dewey and who helped spread it like so much treacle over an apathetic land.

You've heard of method acting. Well, this was method teaching.

Every five years or so, someone would come up with a new gimmick. The great mountain of organized Education would go into prolonged labor. Smoke and flames would emerge from its peak. Tremors and rumblings would shake the countryside. At last the product of all this commotion would be duly born, squeaking a little, it is true, but nonetheless labeled the answer to the profession's prayers.

Back in the mid-1940s there was Platoon Teaching, where one had to go around with a slide rule measuring cubic feet of floor space, and where the Notre Dame Shift could have been used as a model for class scheduling.

Around 1950, Group Dynamics came down like a wolf on the fold, and its cohorts—though not exactly gleaming in purple and gold—managed to dazzle us all with their inside knowledge of such esoteric terms as "discussion leaders," "interrogators," and "research persons."

Education in those halcyon days was stratified in a manner reminiscent of nothing so much as the Hindu caste system. At the bottom—and I will go out of my way to avoid the term "Untouchables"—were the lowly, brainwashed Teachers, of which I was one. On the next rung up the ladder were the Supervisors and Principals, bright-eyed and bushy-tailed, then as now. Then came the "experts" of the many county offices of education, diligently and happily spreading misinformation through their "institutes" and "workshops." The Brahmins in the hierarchy were the professors of education and the myriad consultants and coordinators of the several state departments of education. The whole immense structure towered up like Babel, wreathed in incense fumes, resounding with the chant of the faithful, and supported by the public purse.

Unlike the caste system, of course, there was movement both up and down the ladder. Every so often a teacher became a principal, but only after satisfying the high Brahmins through summer sessions *ad nauseam* and credentials painfully come by. Principals likewise became superintendents, usually after their predecessors had died, either actually or professionally. And superintendents who had been fired for incompetence or who had resigned because of occupational shell shock nearly always ended up as state department of education division heads or as assistant professors of education.

There was movement the other way, too. Anyone who lost control of himself long enough to voice even the mildest protest or to disagree with the professional Pippa's chorus of "God's in His Heaven, all's right with the world" moved down the ladder, and eventually off the ladder altogether.

There were curriculum gimmicks, too. Correlation, for example, blended gracefully into Integration (the non-Southern variety, of course), which in turn flowered spectacularly in the form of Fusion. Somewhere along the line there was even something called Orchestration, which was a refinement of the Core Curriculum and which was supposed to be the ultimate of subtle mingling and mangling and hamburgerizing and homogenizing of various subjects into one steaming, bubbling, nauseous witches' brew.

The absolute quintessence of Good Teaching was supposed to be the combining of every subject area under the sun into a single "unit." "The Westward Movement," for instance. The history part dealt with Dan'l Boone and Davy Crockett, naturally. Geography we taught by tracing the course of the covered wagons as they lumbered through the Cumberland Gap. Science was a little harder to work into the act, the pioneers not being especially known for their contributions in this field, but we managed at least to demonstrate the action of flint on steel as Dan'l lit his pipe while waiting for the Indians to attack. Music was easy. We taught our unfortunate pupils the whining, monotonous folk songs of the Kentucky hillbillies, thus giving rise in more recent years to that supreme American contribution to Twentieth-Century music—Rock 'n' Roll.

English I shudder even to think about, but we made shift

to teach some spelling through the medium of such vital, meaningful "unit" words as *charivari, Conestoga, matchlock*—important words like these. I remember one teacher who was the envy of our whole faculty. She had succeeded in working home economics into "The Westward Movement." She and her class spent an entire week making soap out of ashes, just the way the pioneer women did. Another teaching a unit on Alaska persuaded the school district to get him an electric range so that he and his class could bake sourdough biscuits in honor of the Yukon trailblazers. And so it went.

Poor old Subject Matter, though! Undervalued, despised, kicked into the gutter and left to shift for itself. "Adjustment to the peer group"—that was our watchword. Teach only those things that were "meaningful" to the majority of the pupils. Have them use their hands, even if they needed so desperately to learn to use their heads. Hammers and saws. Construction units. Those were the things!

Ah, but those other things—the things the children never learned from us. The cold, clear beauty of Euclid; the tingling patriotism which Longfellow wrote into the midnight ride of Paul Revere; King Lear out on the heath, defying the fury of Fate and the roaring of the elements; the fascination of the star-dusted light years that stretch from green earth to far Centaurus—what were all those wonderful, magical things to us compared to "educating the whole child," "meeting felt needs," and—of course— "bridging the gap?"

But after all these harsh things have been said about my profession, is it entirely to blame for this generation of folly?

Before our country's educational program can shift gears and move out of the Era of Wonderful Nonsense where it has been for so long, it will be necessary for the plain, ordinary citizen to decide exactly what he wants his schools to do.

Does he want them to be penal institutions, riding herd on entirely too many leather-jacketed, sideburned, duck-tailed individuals who hate Education in any form, delight in running teachers out of their classrooms, and make it impossible for the vast majority of normal, decent kids to learn anything? Because that's what a lot of schools are right now. . . .

Does he want them to act as lay churches, teaching the children to distinguish among the creeds and heresies of Christian dogma, Judaic morality, and atheistic dialectic? Should educators become Bible readers, scriptural commentators, and theological torchbearers in an age of vice and gross materialism? Because that's what a good many folks want us to do. . . .

Does he want the schools to take over the duties of hospitals and clinics? To feed and clothe children whose parents—many of them—have decided that it's easier to let the schools do it? To entertain the younger generation with organized recreation administered and financed by the schools? Because—once again—that's what a lot of us are doing. . . .

Or does our hypothetical average citizen want the schools to go back to doing what schools have done since the days of Plato and Aristotle and before—to serve as the cultural bastions of a society beleaguered by the forces of crass materialism, to hand down from generation to generation the hard-won, dearly-bought tools of intellectual supremacy forged by our forebears with such infinite pains in the crucible of genius? Does he want the schools, in brief, to *teach*? I say that he does—and that the people of the United States do.

Within the last year or two, we have witnessed the beginning of the Conservative Revolution in Education. Children are being grouped according to their abilities. Home work is being assigned to elementary children. Foreign languages are being taught down in the grades. Eighth graders are studying Latin and algebra. Kindergarteners in a few places are even being taught to read. In California, teachers must now have an academic major or minor before they can qualify for credentials.

Mark this: until just the other day, *all these things were considered heresy by my profession.*

But although much has been accomplished, infinitely more remains to be done.

The terms "social studies" and "language arts" should be relegated to the scrap heap reserved for outworn cliches like "Twenty-three skidoo!" and "Oh, you kid!"

Our schools should require instruction in ancient, medieval, modern, and American history starting in the lower grades and going right through high school.

Comprehensive knowledge of world and American geography should be expected of all children of normal intelligence, and taught them in a systematized form.

Class work should include in all schools memorization and drill in vital subjects, such as historical dates and names of great significance, the multiplication tables and number combinations, and passages from great works of prose and poetry so that the next generation will not inherit the cultural vacuum which we have inflicted upon the present one.

The schools—all of them—should teach the basic principles of our American free enterprise system, contrasting modern democratic capitalism point by point with totalitarian Communism and its system of complete control.

None of these things are being done today except in a relatively few schools.

When all these goals are reached—when standards in English and science and mathematics have been raised to the point where they will demand the best efforts of every student, when teachers and school administrators are required to pass examinations in subject matter dealing with our cultural heritage as they are now required to do in educational methods and psychology—then and only then will we have Education for Survival.

This, then, is Survivalism. It is designed to preserve our birthright and to give us the tools to protect it. Unless we accept it, or something very like it, in another generation we shall not have a country to defend, and someone else will be educating our children's children.

Nothing is more vital than this question, because on it hangs the future itself. Only through the adoption of Survivalism as its official philosophy can Education once again assume in our land its rightful status.

It would be improper to leave with the reader the aftervision of Education as a kind of snake pit wherein Progressives grapple with Conservatives amid the depressing thud of crashing standards. If it were no more than this, the profession would long since have pulled down the pillars of the temple upon its own head.

But in no other calling do the tides of life sweep in and out so ceaselessly, so colorfully. And once in a great passage of time, the tides bring in a specimen of jetsam so sparkling and so strange as to reconcile the practitioner of our great, complex Art to all its heartbreak and perversity. . . .

The Day the Prince Dropped In

13

As I LOOK back upon my sole encounter with royalty, the whole affair takes on the stark yet dreamlike lines of a primitive Gold Coast carving. I could have sworn that my profession had armored me beyond the possibility of surprise, but Prince Mwuabistia surprised me. This is too mild. He entranced me.

All kinds of people walk into my office. As a public servant, I have cultivated a response appropriate to each type. The irate taxpayer gets my "Gad-but-I'm-busy-but-I'll-find-time-for-*you*" look. The school board member rates my "Things-are-chugging-along-nicely" face, and such lesser forms of life as supply salesmen and job applicants have to get along with variations on my "Life-is-real-life-is-earnest" expression.

Nothing in my experience, however, had prepared me for the day the Prince dropped in.

An assistant had stuck his head in at the door with a somewhat bemused expression.

"We have a visitor I think you will want to see," he had announced tentatively, and suddenly I found myself shaking hands with my first prince. None of my expressions seemed at all appropriate somehow.

My guest introduced himself somewhat apologetically,

as though embarrassed at his intrusion. He spoke beautiful English in an accent redolent of Oxford and in deep organ tones that contrasted pitilessly with my flat Western ones.

"I want to assure you that this sort of impromptu calling is not at all my cup of tea," he smiled, "but I do happen to be in a bit of a dilemma. It might be as well if you were to look over my bona fides before I go on."

He extracted a sheaf of documents from an attaché case and handed them to me. I leafed through them, looking up from time to time as I came upon identification photos or descriptions. As he leaned back in one of my office chairs, my visitor was a striking young man of medium height, well groomed, and dressed in the latest American sports clothes.

His alien registration forms seemed in order. They identified the bearer as Mwuabistia Nkabouri Kaunstiorri, Crown Prince of the Ubangi-Shari nation and heir to the throne of what was at that time a French Equatorial African possession. Other papers testified to his residence in Palo Alto, where he was pursuing graduate studies at Stanford. Letters from several college deans, chamber of commerce presidents, and chiefs of police in three states attested warmly to the Prince's ability as a lecturer.

I handed back the documents.

"We're delighted to have you with us, Your Highness. You mentioned a problem?"

The prince smiled ruefully, and proceeded to explain. He had been en route by bus to the coast from a speaking engagement at a New Mexico college when his wallet had been lifted during a breakfast stop. His Highness was annoyed, but tolerant. Pickpockets, it seems, are unknown in his country.

"However," he hastened to add, "when and if our people acquire pockets, doubtless the pickpockets will follow as a matter of course."

Nevertheless, it was necessary to cable his father's finance minister in Brazzaville for more funds. Inasmuch as he was in the United States as a student, he had come to my office for help in sending the cable.

It is not every day that an opportunity is afforded to help a prince in distress. Within the hour, the message had been financed, overnight lodgings had been arranged with the local minister of the prince's faith, and I had had the pleasure of His Highness's company at lunch.

His expression of gratitude was reserved but genuine. He assured me of a right royal welcome should I ever find myself in his native land, a contingency which seemed to me somewhat remote. Meanwhile, he asked if I would be interested in hearing something of his country. Needless to say, I was, and entered as easily as this upon the most amazing hour I have ever spent.

It was apparent from his first words that I was hosting a master storyteller. Outside my window, the endless vistas and lunar landscape of the great Mojave stretched as majestically as before, but as I listened to my guest, the white-hot sunlight dappled to a lush green. The whine of the desert wind blended imperceptibly into the myriad chatterings and trumpetings of the primeval jungle, and the ubiquitous sand gave way to swaying foliage. Africa, incongruously and inescapably, invaded my humble office.

He spoke of great rivers, magnificent mountains looming like ghosts out of the Sahara far to the north, strange beasts and people.

"It's a mistake, you know, about our lips. The Ubangi

have not practiced lip stretching for more than a generation, and even then the 'plate lips' were being perpetuated by white promoters. Originally—long ago—the deformation originated as a successful attempt to protect the women of my nation from the ravages of slave traders."

Prince Mwuabistia paused, and spoke simply.

"Our women today are as God made them. They walk beneath our great trees as Eve must have walked, queenly and unafraid. They are beautiful."

He took color photos from his briefcase. Some were of the royal family. He pointed proudly to the magnificently proportioned King, his father. His eyes softened as he indicated the kindly features of his mother.

"Most of my people are Christians. The rest are Moslems. For many years we have lived together in peace. There is no warfare and little crime among the Ubangi. So much in harmony are they with the nature in whose midst they live that strife is alien to them, something outside their comprehension. They have solved the problem that eats at the world's heart."

My visitor's face glowed whenever he spoke of his people. He told of their marriage customs and their strangely touching betrothal rites, with the maiden's closing admonition, "Be thou lord in my hut and chieftain of my spirit, that I may walk unafraid through the jungle of life."

He recited pasages from *The Broken Spear*, the booming ritual chanted at the bedside of the dying which girds the soul for its journey through the Hereafter and which bears a marked resemblance to the classical Egyptian *Book of the Dead*.

As the organ tones rose and fell, I sensed a stir outside my open door. Clerks and typists from the outer offices were finding excuses to move into hearing range. The Prince, back for a little space with his own kind, never noticed.

"North of my father's capital at Bambari is the Stone of Sacrifice, jutting from the swamps of the Dar Rounga. A century ago, before the French came, the first Christian missionary to our land broke the power of the royal witch doctors there. Massive as a great building, the Stone towers above the flatness of the surrounding country. It is rich in iron ore, a natural target for the lightning which has scarred and blackened it over the ages."

The knot of listeners was growing by the minute.

"The court magician challenged the alien prophet to a duel atop the Stone, where rebels and men of violence had been hurled to their doom for unnumbered generations. The weapons were to be the frightful bolts of electricity which ripened in the womb of the black storm clouds even then sweeping in from the far-off ranges of the Jebel Marra. The prize, the souls of my people."

Outside, the desert sun still shone, but we who listened could almost hear the mutter of the approaching thunder.

"The two men climbed painfully to the mesalike summit of the Stone, each facing the other across fifty feet of flattened rock. Around them the storm broke, and the waters came down. The ravening fires of heaven crashed around them. The king's wizard stamped his feet and called upon the gods of the jungle. The stranger prayed to Jesus. Those who watched from afar saw the Stone blaze all over, as though dipped in a sea of flame. At last, the bearer of the Christ-news came down, slowly and painfully as he had gone up. The other did not come down, then or ever."

The Prince rose and offered his hand, smiling cheerfully.

"There has been but one God for the Ubangi-Shari since that day. May He be with you, my friend."

The knot outside my door untied itself quickly as our visitor took his leave. Things went back to normal, but the tempo was somehow quickened and increased.

I leaned back in my chair. For a brief hour, I had poled my way upstream to the sources of the Nana Bakasso. I had lost myself in the emerald woodlands of the Oubangui, and hunted leopards in the Massif de Tondou. I could have listened, I told myself wonderingly, all day.

That was the first time I met the Prince and heard him talk.

The second and last time I met him, he was in jail. And he wasn't talking.

The next morning I received a phone call from our local police chief.

"I'm entertaining a friend of yours down here," he chuckled. I came right down.

Eventually I had to admit that I had been taken. But at first, even after I had heard the chief's report and read the teletypes, I could hardly believe it. Prince Mwuabistia, of course, turned out to be plain Edward Smith, or Jones, depending upon which set of bulletins I cared to credit. Born in Florida and never outside the United States, he had operated widely for more than three years. In that time, he had managed to "borrow" quite a bit of money to send those cables to Brazzaville. Stanford had never heard of him. A good many police departments had, however.

I glared at the grinning chief.

"What about his papers? The letters from the colleges? His family pictures?"

It was no use. The prince had faked them all. All, that is, but the letters. They were genuine enough, but those who had written them now wished they hadn't. I, it seemed, was not the only one who had been induced to pole up the Nana Bakasso.

The only question left was, "Why?" and I asked it. My friend's grin vanished. He rubbed his nose.

"That's the funny part of the whole deal. The time and trouble he must have taken to build up the background of this hoax just aren't justified by the money he got out of it. The information I have from the other cities where His Highness operated is that he never got away with much more than traveling money, and most of that was in the form of ten-dollar 'loans.' "

The chief pawed through his teletypes. He raised his eyebrows.

"I've got lots of warnings to look out for him, but nary a hold order. Nobody seems to want to prosecute. Do you want me to book him for impersonation?"

I shook my head.

"Okay, okay." The chief was mildly annoyed. "Now you tell *me* why."

I got up and walked to the door. Beyond it was the corridor leading to the cell block. At the far end, gazing tranquilly through the bars, the Prince looked at me. After a long moment, he smiled and nodded. I turned back.

"Maybe it's because you just don't jail royalty."

That evoked nothing but a disgusted snort. My own feelings were hard to analyze. I only knew that the idea of the Prince behind bars triggered a feeling of incongruity. I kept telling myself in vain that everything my visitor had told me about the Ubangi had originated in libraries which he had haunted. The religious rites had come out of his imagination, and the lightning duel out of the pages of Rider Haggard. It was no use. I couldn't work up anything more than a vague sense of regret.

The truth, or a portion of it, came to me a short time later as I watched the silent figure hiking out of town. The radiograms and teletypes had been wrong. Oh, years ago, perhaps, a man named Smith or Jones or Brown had embarked upon a masquerade. He had borrowed majesty and gone forth into a world where a title was a touchstone to acceptance. But in learning his role, little by little he had lost his original identity. A far-off land which he had never seen had become more real to him than his own, which had rejected him. He had fallen in love with a mirage which daily clothed itself more solidly in soil and rock and living creatures. And, in the end, he had become a prince indeed.

More, he had struck a chord deep-buried in the hearts of all of us. From town to dusty town he wandered, telling again and again the story which had become his life. Living it as he had come to do, he made it live also for those who listened to him. Shimmering in the jungle sunshine, the private world of Prince Mwuabistia sparked into momentary flame the *fata morgana* which each of us carries within him.

No wonder we had refused to prosecute. A dream is not for jailing.

As I looked after him, the distant figure rounded the bend and slipped from sight. I could not help but feel that some day, in his own time and his own way, the Prince would go beyond the headwaters of the Bar Rounga to that magic spot where, gazing across half Africa, he might glimpse above the horizon the Mountains of the Moon.